## PEOPLE
### IN THE NEWS

# Lance Armstrong

## by John F. Grabowski

**LUCENT BOOKS**

*An imprint of Thomson Gale, a part of The Thomson Corporation*

THOMSON
™
GALE

Detroit • New York • San Francisco • San Diego • New Haven, Conn.
Waterville, Maine • London • Munich

© 2005 Thomson Gale, a part of The Thomson Corporation.

Thomson and Star Logo are trademarks and Gale and Lucent Books are registered trademarks used herein under license.

For more information, contact
Lucent Books
27500 Drake Rd.
Farmington Hills, MI 48331-3535
Or you can visit our Internet site at http://www.gale.com

LIBRARY OF CONGRESS CATALOGING-IN-PUBLICATION DATA

Grabowski, John F.
  Lance Armstrong / by John F. Grabowski.
    p. cm. — (People in the news)
  Includes bibliographical references and index.
  ISBN 1-59018-711-3 (hard cover : alk. paper)
  1. Armstrong, Lance—Juvenile literature. 2. Cyclists—United States—Biography—Juvenile literature. 3. Cancer—Patients—United States—Biography—Juvenile literature. I. Title. II. Series: People in the news (San Diego, Calif.)
  GV1051.A76G73 2005
  796.6'2'092—dc22

                                                                    2004028565

Printed in the United States of America

# Table of Contents

# Foreword

Fame and celebrity are alluring. People are drawn to those who walk in fame's spotlight, whether they are known for great accomplishments or for notorious deeds. The lives of the famous pique public interest and attract attention, perhaps because their experiences seem in some ways so different from, yet in other ways so similar to, our own.

Newspapers, magazines, and television regularly capitalize on this fascination with celebrity by running profiles of famous people. For example, television programs such as *Entertainment Tonight* devote all of their programming to stories about entertainment and entertainers. Magazines such as *People* fill their pages with stories of the private lives of famous people. Even newspapers, newsmagazines, and television news frequently delve into the lives of well-known personalities. Despite the number of articles and programs, few provide more than a superficial glimpse at their subjects.

Lucent's People in the News series offers young readers a deeper look into the lives of today's news makers, the influences that have shaped them, and the impact they have had in their fields of endeavor and on other people's lives. The subjects of the series hail from many disciplines and walks of life. They include authors, musicians, athletes, political leaders, entertainers, entrepreneurs, and others who have made a mark on modern life and who, in many cases, will continue to do so for years to come.

These biographies are more than factual chronicles. Each book emphasizes the contributions, accomplishments, or deeds that have brought fame or notoriety to the individual and shows how that person has influenced modern life. Authors portray their subjects in a realistic, unsentimental light. For example, Bill Gates—the cofounder and chief executive officer of the software giant Microsoft—has been instrumental in making personal computers the most vital tool of the modern age. Few dispute his business savvy, his perseverance, or his technical expertise, yet critics say he is ruthless in his dealings with competitors and driven more by his desire to maintain Microsoft's dominance in the computer industry than by an interest in furthering technology.

In these books, young readers will encounter inspiring stories about real people who achieved success despite enormous obstacles. Oprah Winfrey—the most powerful, most watched, and wealthiest woman on television today—spent the first six years of her life in the care of her grandparents while her unwed mother sought work and a better life elsewhere. Her adolescence was colored by promiscuity, pregnancy at age fourteen, rape, and sexual abuse.

Each author documents and supports his or her work with an array of primary and secondary source quotations taken from diaries, letters, speeches, and interviews. All quotes are footnoted to show readers exactly how and where biographers derive their information and provide guidance for further research. The quotations enliven the text by giving readers eyewitness views of the life and accomplishments of each person covered in the People in the News series.

In addition, each book in the series includes photographs, annotated bibliographies, timelines, and comprehensive indexes. For both the casual reader and the student researcher, the People in the News series offers insight into the lives of today's news makers—people who shape the way we live, work, and play in the modern age.

# Introduction

# A Life Fulfilled

CYCLING AT ITS highest level is one of the most grueling of all sports, and one event is considered cycling's most grueling contest. The Tour de France is the sport's Super Bowl, its World Series, its Stanley Cup championship. For three weeks, racers pedal across more than 2,000 miles (3,219km) of countryside, bicycling up and down hills and mountains in all kinds of weather, at speeds approaching seventy miles an hour. Lance Armstrong, the man who has won this punishing contest more times than anyone, believes the Tour de France transcends athleticism:

> It's a metaphor for life, not only the longest race in the world but also the most exalting and heartbreaking and potentially tragic.
>
> [The Tour de France] poses every conceivable element to the rider, and more: cold, heat, mountains, plains, ruts, flat tires, high winds, unspeakably bad luck, unthinkable beauty, yawning senselessness, and above all a great, deep self-questioning. During our lives we're faced with so many different elements as well, we experience so many setbacks, and fight such a hand-to-hand battle with failure, head down in the rain, just trying to stay upright and to have a little hope. The Tour is not just a bike race, not at all. It is a test. It tests you physically, it tests you mentally, and it even tests you morally.[1]

In 1999 Armstrong became the second American to win that grueling test. Then the brash young man from Plano, Texas, proceeded to collect a string of victories, winning the Tour for the next five years for an unprecedented six victories. His feat broke the record of five Tour victories previously held by Europeans

Jacques Anquetil, Eddy Merckx, Bernard Hinault, and Miguel Induráin. A turn of phrase used by fans and headline writers everywhere succinctly captured Armstrong's dominance of the world's most revered biking race in a memorable three-syllable pun: Tour de Lance.

Armstrong's triumphs on the roads of France, however, have not been his biggest victories. In 1996, at the age of twenty-five,

*Six-time Tour de France winner and cancer survivor Lance Armstrong celebrates as he wins the fifteenth stage of the 2004 Tour de France.*

he was diagnosed with testicular cancer, which had spread to his chest and brain. Some doctors estimated his chance of survival at less than 20 percent. Despite this poor prognosis, Armstrong made a miraculous recovery and defeated the disease.

Armstrong went on to become a legend in and beyond sports. In 2004 a *Sports Illustrated* fan poll voted him the "All-Time Greatest Sportsman" ahead of Michael Jordan, Muhammad Ali, and many other great athletes in sports with far higher profiles than professional bicycling. Armstrong's ability to conquer his disease despite overwhelming odds inspires cancer patients all around the world. He proves that cancer does not have to mean a death sentence and that survivors can continue to lead productive, fulfilling lives. He champions the cause of cancer survivorship through his Lance Armstrong Foundation and offers hope and inspiration through the sheer power of his personal story.

"Lance is convinced had he never had cancer he may never have won the oldest, longest, and hardest bicycle race here on earth,"[2] Linda Armstrong Kelly, his mother, has said. At every opportunity she preached key words of wisdom to her son. Time and again she told him, "Turn an obstacle into an opportunity. Turn a negative into a positive."[3] Armstrong managed to turn the obstacle of all obstacles, a life-threatening illness, into an opportunity that set the stage for his unprecedented cycling victories and served as the seed for a foundation that has helped countless cancer survivors. His actions are the ultimate expression of his mother's sage advice.

# Chapter 1

---

# Childhood in Plano

Lance Armstrong was born Lance Gunderson on September 18, 1971, in Oak Cliff, Texas—a middle-class suburb of Dallas perhaps best known as the final resting place of gangster Clyde Barrow and the town where Lee Harvey Oswald was captured following the assassination of President John F. Kennedy. Lance's mother, Linda Mooneyham, was just seventeen years old when she gave birth to him. "My mother never went to college and had no opportunities," recalls Armstrong. "When she had me, she was up against the wall. People said her life was over."[4]

Lance never knew his father, a man named Eddie Gunderson, who married Linda on her seventeenth birthday. The marriage did not last long, and the couple divorced before Lance was two years old. To this day Armstrong has remained estranged from his biological father. "I never knew my so-called father. He was a non-factor—unless you count his absence as a factor. Just because he provided the DNA that made me doesn't make him my father, and as far as I'm concerned, there is nothing between us, absolutely no connection."[5]

Armstrong credits all he has accomplished to his mother. She returned to school to get her diploma after he was born, then worked a series of jobs to help support her family. She always sought to improve their lives. "When I used to babysit," she recalled, "I'd be in this nice home, and I'd say, 'One of these days I'm going to have that.' I wanted something more. I had every excuse to fail, but I was obsessed."[6] Linda eventually got a job as a secretary that enabled her to move with Lance to a nicer apartment in Richardson, just north of Dallas.

When Lance was three, his mother married a traveling sales-
man named Terry Armstrong. Armstrong adopted the youngster,
giving him his name. With a second income added to the house-
hold, Linda was able to afford a new home in Plano, a more ex-
clusive suburb of Dallas.

Ultimately this second marriage also failed. Armstrong, a born-
again Christian, was a strict disciplinarian. He often used a pad-
dle on Lance for relatively minor misdeeds, such as being messy
or sloppy. Lance did not like his stepfather, and he was not unhappy when the marriage broke up. "He was totally unfair to
my mother,"[7] he recalled years later.

*Armstrong attributes his life's success to his mother, Linda. Here, Armstrong*
*celebrates victory in the nineteenth stage of the 1999 Tour de France with her.*

## A Missing Father

In July 1999 the Austin *American-Statesman* published an article on Armstrong's biological father, Eddie Gunderson. Armstrong has not had any contact with Gunderson, who works for the *Dallas Morning News,* since he was three years old. According to the article by John Maher, Gunderson made an unsuccessful attempt to find Armstrong in the mid-1990s. Said Gunderson, "I had it in my mind that I'd walk right up and say, 'I'm Eddie Gunderson, your biological father.' But had I found [his house], well, I don't know. That's the closest I ever came."

Shortly after Gunderson and Lance's mother, Linda, divorced, he fell behind on his twenty-dollar-a-week child support payments. He did not protest when Linda's second husband, Terry Armstrong, legally adopted Lance. Gunderson feared he would be jailed for the missed payments. "What I did was crazy," admits Gunderson. "I was pretty wild when I was young. I'm sure she's told him a lot of things about me, and I'm sure most of the things she told him are true. His mom is his biggest fan, and she's done an excellent job."

Following the divorce, Lance grew closer than ever to his mother. He helped out around the house whenever he could. Linda, for her part, allowed him to exercise his independence and youthful exuberance. "I have loved him every minute of his life," she said, "but, God, there were times when it was a struggle."[8]

Linda always encouraged Lance to do his best no matter what he did. When she came home one night, frustrated after a difficult day at work, he asked her why she did not quit. "Son," she replied, "you never quit."[9] Lance never forgot her words.

## Early Interests

When Lance's family lived in Richardson, their apartment was across the street from a store called the Richardson Bike Mart. The owner, Jim Hoyt, sponsored bike races in the area, and he took an interest in young Lance. When the youngster was seven years old, Hoyt sold him his first serious bike: a brown Schwinn Mag Scrambler. Lance loved the bike, which to him represented independence. "A bike is freedom to roam," he recalled, "without rules and without adults."[10]

In addition to cycling, Lance also developed interests in running and swimming. He won his first distance-running race when he was in the fifth grade. Soon after, his mother enrolled him in the City of Plano Swim Club. He did not do well at first, but he was determined to succeed. Chris MacCurdy, his coach, put him on a strict training schedule, with workouts every morning from 5:30 to 7:00. The results were impressive. Within a year, Lance was fourth in the state in the 1,500-meter freestyle event.

As Lance got older his swimming regimen had the added benefit of helping him improve as a cyclist. He rode his bike 10 miles (16km) to the pool in the morning, and then swam 4,000 meters (approximately 2.5 miles) of laps before school. After classes ended, he returned to the swim club for another two-hour, 6,000-meter (3.75-mile) workout. Then he mounted his bike for the 10-mile (16km) ride home. The 6 miles (9.6km) a day in the water and the 20 miles (32km) a day on the bike was a grueling routine for a twelve-year-old. His work quickly paid off. He developed into one of the best athletes in his age group in the city.

## The Triathlete

When Lance was thirteen, he learned of a junior triathlon competition called IronKids. It was the first time he had heard of the triathlon, an event that combines biking, swimming, and running— three sports at which Lance excelled. He entered the event with his mother's blessing. Without any special training, he proceeded to win the IronKids by a comfortable margin. Lance followed up his victory with another win in a triathlon in Houston.

Lance's successes proved profitable, as well as confidence building, as he began pocketing checks for his wins. He soon moved up to events against older, more experienced athletes. He entered the 1987 President's Triathlon and finished in thirty-second place, a remarkable feat for a fifteen-year-old. The following year, *Triathlete* magazine named him "National Rookie of the Year," noting that he could become "one of the greatest athletes the sport has ever seen." [11]

While he was competing in triathlons, Lance was also making a name for himself in local bike races. He began in Category 4 races—the lowest category—but soon moved up. He quickly became convinced he had a future as a professional athlete. He developed a new obsession: becoming a world-class athlete.

Lance's exercise regimen helped him develop physically. "At age 13, 14, those years when your body develops and you go through so much growth, I was swimming 10,000 meters a day," he said. "That's all upper-body work, so you can imagine that when I was 14 years old I was this incredibly buffed-out little kid. Not the Hulk but definitely bulky." [12]

When he was sixteen, one clue to the sources of Lance's superior athleticism surfaced in a test he took. Michael Specter described the test in an article in the *New Yorker:*

> [At age sixteen], he was invited to the Cooper Institute, in Dallas, which was one of the first centers to recognize the relationship between fitness and aerobic conditioning. Everyone uses oxygen to break down food into the components that provide energy; the more oxygen you are able to use, the more energy you will produce, and the faster you can run, ride, or swim. Armstrong was given a

*Already a seasoned triathlete at the age of seventeen, Armstrong puts on his wetsuit at the start of the 1988 Jeep Triathlon Grand Prix, a professional race.*

test called the VO2 Max, which is commonly used to assess an athlete's aerobic ability: it measures the maximum amount of oxygen the lungs can consume during exercise. His levels were the highest ever recorded at the clinic.[13]

## The Risk Taker

Lance had always been a risk taker whose behavior sometimes got him into trouble. As a boy, he invented a dangerous activity he called fireball. It involved soaking a tennis ball in kerosene, lighting it with a match, and playing catch with it while wearing a pair of padded garden gloves. On one occasion his "game" almost had tragic consequences. The burning ball landed on the roof of his house, ignited some shingles, and almost set the house on fire.

His risky behavior extended to his bike riding. Lance would speed through stoplights at intersections, tempting fate. Once he was badly injured when he was blindsided by a woman whose car hit him as he shot across a highway. This love of speed followed him through school. While at Plano East High School, he competed in drag races in the Chevy Camaro IROC Z28 that Hoyt helped him obtain.

### Hometown of a Champion

Plano, Texas, is a city of 243,000 people located in Collin County, a farm and livestock area on the blackland prairie approximately twenty miles north of downtown Dallas. The community originated in the early 1840s and was settled by pioneers who migrated from Kentucky and Tennessee. It received the name Plano, meaning "plain" or "flatland" in Spanish, around 1850, and was incorporated twenty-three years later.

For much of its existence, Plano relied on the surrounding farms and ranches for its livelihood. The growth of nearby Dallas in the 1960s attracted several technology firms, which had a positive influence on the local economy. By the 1970s, Plano had become one of the fastest-growing cities in the nation. In January 2004, CNN Money named Plano as its top place to live in the western United States (of cities with a population of more than 100,000).

Although Lance's success as a swimmer and triathlete helped him win some friends and become accepted at Plano East, he still felt like an outsider at times. He believed that many of his peers looked down on him because of his lower-middle-class upbringing. And winning triathlons did not make him a star athlete with legions of adoring fans. Plano, like most Texas towns, revered just one sport: football. Lance had no aptitude for the sport. "I wasn't any good at football," he recalled. "No speed, no coordination." [14]

Lance's involvement in cycling eventually caused him problems in school. During the second half of his senior year, he was invited by the U.S. Cycling Federation to train with the junior U.S. national team in Colorado Springs. There he would prepare for the 1990 Junior World Championships, which were to be held in Moscow. The administration at Plano East frowned on the trip, citing the school's policy on unexcused absences. Lance decided to go anyway.

He impressed the U.S. Cycling Federation officials at the Junior World Championships, including the Russian coach, who praised him as one of the top young cyclists he had ever seen. The administration at Plano East, however, was upset. When Lance returned after the six-week sojourn, he and his mother were told he would not be allowed to graduate with his class unless he made up all the work he had missed in the few weeks that remained. Lance was devastated.

His mother came to his rescue by finding a private academy—Bending Oaks—that was willing to accept him. Following his mother's lead, Lance transferred his credits from Plano East, took a couple of makeup courses, and graduated on time.

## Europe Beckons

Following his graduation, Armstrong competed in bike races around the country for a trade team sponsored by Subaru-Montgomery. He also kept in contact with Hoyt, who encouraged him—and other young riders in the area—by providing him with equipment and paying him stipends for his performance in local races.

In one Tuesday-night criterium (multilap road race), Armstrong had a confrontation with another rider. The two bicyclists began

*Initially, Armstrong's youthful arrogance and love of speed angered his coaches.*

throwing punches as soon as the race was over, and they wound up sprawled in the dirt on top of one another. Furious with Armstrong's behavior, Hoyt picked up his bike and wheeled it away. When Lance went to Hoyt's home to retrieve it, the irate man refused to give it to him. "You want to talk to me," he said, "you come to my office tomorrow."[15] Like many youngsters his age, Armstrong could be very stubborn. He refused to apologize to his benefactor.

The situation became more aggravated several days later. Unhappy with Armstrong's habit of speeding around town in the Camaro, Hoyt also took back the car. (Although Armstrong made the payments on the car, Hoyt's sponsorship was his main source of income. In addition, Hoyt had arranged for the loan.) Armstrong's anger at—and fear of—the man caused a rift that lasted for years.

The run-in with Hoyt led Armstrong to make a decision he had pondered for some time. Although he had achieved considerable success in his cycling ventures, he knew that serious riders eventually gravitated to Europe, where the sport was extremely popular. To become a world-class rider, he knew he needed experience in international competition.

Following the Junior World Championships in Moscow in 1990, Armstrong had been named to the U.S. national cycling team. At that time Chris Carmichael, the team's director, had invited Lance and other young cyclists to accompany him to Europe. Carmichael wanted to raise the standards of U.S. riders, and he thought they would realize their potential by competing with the Europeans, regarded as the world's best cyclists. With his relationship with Hoyt at a low point, Armstrong knew the time was right for him to accept Carmichael's invitation.

Unlike many parents, who might have been against such a move, Linda did not stand in her son's way. "I could have been all over his case about going to college," she recalled. "He had scholarship offers in swimming. But I always told him to follow his heart." [16]

## Learning How to Ride

Despite his enormous potential, the brash youngster still had a lot to learn. His youthful arrogance, however, made it difficult for him to accept this. Armstrong's first impulse in racing had always been to attack fast and early, with no concern for strategy. Recalled Carmichael:

> I had never met him when I took over as coach. I called him up and we talked on the phone. He was kind of rude. Not kind of rude. He was completely rude. He was, like, "So you are the new coach—what are you going to teach me?" . . . I would tell him to wait till the end of a race before making a break. He just couldn't do that. He would get out in front and set the pace. He would burn up the field, and when other riders came alive he would be done, spent. [17]

Such tactics were a hindrance in international competition. In Armstrong's first big international race—the 1990 amateur World Championships in Utsunomiya, Japan—he managed to finish in eleventh place, at that time the highest ever by an American. Still, Carmichael criticized him for starting out fast instead of drafting (following close behind another cyclist in his slipstream, or air pocket, to allow the following rider to expend less energy). "If you had known what you were doing and conserved your energy," he told him, "you'd have been in the medals." [18] Carmichael also encouraged Armstrong, however, telling him he could someday be a world champion if he worked hard enough and learned his craft. Carmichael convinced him that at this level of competition, tactics and strategy played important parts in the race, as much as strength and endurance.

Armstrong's plan was to race as an amateur through 1992. After the Olympics in Barcelona, Spain, that summer, he intended to turn professional. In the meantime he was making a name for himself as one of the best young racers around. His win in the prestigious Settimana Bergamasca in Italy was an impressive victory for the American program, coming as it did against some of the best Italian pros. It did not sit especially well with some of the hometown fans, however. Incensed that an American was leading the race, some threw shattered glass and thumbtacks in the road, hoping that Armstrong would blow a tire. Most of the spectators, however, soon warmed to the American with the hard-riding style.

## Turning Pro

Armstrong won the U.S. Amateur Championship in 1991 and looked forward to making a strong showing in the Barcelona Olympics. He had some impressive successes in the first half of 1992, winning high-profile races in Spain (La Vuelta La Ribiera), Atlanta (the First Union Grand Prix), and Pittsburgh (the Thrift Drug Classic). The Olympics, however, were not what he expected. After finishing second in the U.S. time trials, Armstrong came in a disappointing fourteenth place in Barcelona. Said Carmichael, "Lance had one bad race all year. Unfortunately, it

*A young Armstrong poses in the stars-and-stripes jersey of the U.S. national cycling team before the start of a stage of the 1991 Tour DuPont.*

was the Olympic road race. I'm responsible for it. There was too much preparation and too narrow a focus. We should have treated it like any other race." [19]

However, some observers of Armstrong's career believed that the setback helped him in the long run. Said his friend J.T. Neal, with whom he worked at the time, "Before the 1992 Olympics he thought no one could touch him. It was a sobering experience, part of a maturing process." [20]

# Chapter 2

# A Young Star

IMMEDIATELY FOLLOWING HIS disappointing finish in the Olympics, Armstrong turned professional. Jim Ochowicz, who was the director of a team sponsored by Motorola and comprised mainly of American riders, signed him to his first contract. "Och," as he was called, had been impressed by Armstrong's desire to be a great cyclist. "I want to be the best rider there is," Armstrong had told him when they met. "I want to go to Europe and be a pro. I don't want to just be good at it, I want to be the best."[21]

Armstrong's first race as a professional was the Clásica San Sebastián, a tortuous one-day Spanish race of more than one hundred miles. The race was held in a torrential downpour and many of the riders dropped out before the finish. Remembering his mother's words, however, Armstrong would not quit. He finished in last place out of 111 riders, crossing the finish line nearly half an hour after the leader. It was a humbling experience. "It wasn't as if I was just in last place," he later recalled. "They were taking down the podium and everyone had gone home by the time I reached the finish."[22]

Armstrong began to wonder if he could compete at this level. Depressed, he told Carmichael he was considering quitting and going home. "I thought maybe I wasn't any good," he said. "I thought, 'God, these guys are that much better than me.' It was very humbling."[23] Carmichael talked him out of quitting and praised him for finishing the race at all. With his confidence somewhat restored, Armstrong raced in the Championship of Zurich three days later and finished second. The quick turnaround convinced him he had made the right choice. More and more, people were beginning to talk about the hard-riding American.

## The Etiquette of the Race

Europeans were not used to Armstrong's style of riding. In international cycling competition, riders know that respect for one another can be an important factor in someone's success. There are rules of etiquette that are generally accepted by all racers. For example, team members—and sometimes competitors—often take turns pulling to the front of the pack of riders in order to share the advantages of drafting. The unusual etiquette of cycling insists that an individual rider not take advantage of others in certain situations. If part of the peloton (the main group of riders in a race) is caught at a train crossing, for example, the ones who made it past the train will not push ahead to put time between them and the others. Another unwritten rule prevents someone from breaking away while an opponent stops to urinate.

It is also true in cycling that an individual rider's success depends on the success of the team. The younger members usually start out as *domestiques*—riders who put their success second to that

*During a mountain stage of the 1993 Tour DuPont, Armstrong attacks early, demonstrating the overly aggressive riding style that characterized his early career.*

## A Variety of Races

Bicycle racing may be broken up into four categories: road, track, mountain bike, and cyclo-cross. Armstrong's specialty is road racing, in which riders race along paved roadways. These races may include events such as time trials (where cyclists begin at staggered intervals and race against the clock) and criteriums (multilap races around a short course). Longer events, held over periods ranging from several days to three weeks, are known as stage races.

Track, or velodrome, racing consists of speed events held in close quarters on a banked track. The distances generally range anywhere from 200 meters (219yds) to 4 kilometers (2.5 miles). Track racing was very popular in the 1800s and is making a comeback. At present there are about twenty velodromes in the United States.

*Although Armstrong is known as a road cyclist, here he showcases his skill as a mountain biker in a 1999 race.*

Mountain bike races take place on challenging courses that have been laid out in the wilderness. Relatively new compared to the other forms of cycling, mountain bike races consist of endurance and gravity events. Endurance events include cross-country, short-track, and marathon races; gravity events include downhill, mountain cross, and dual slalom.

Cyclo-cross races are held on relatively short courses that combine runs on grass with short-road or dirt-road sections. The courses contain several human-made barriers at which the bikers must dismount and run over.

of the team leader. In an article in the *New Yorker,* Michael Specter discusses the relationship between the leader and the *domestiques* in the Tour de France:

> Since individual excellence can get one only so far in a race of this magnitude, it is also crucial to have the right team, to provide organization, finances, and experience. [Armstrong's team] U.S. Postal has all that; it is, in its way, pro cycling's

Yankees—with climbing specialists, sprinters, and a powerful bench. This is why so many cyclists agree to work as *domestiques,* putting their success second to Armstrong's. "You work for a teammate who is older and more experienced," [Colombian rider] Victor Hugo Peña told me late one day between stages of the Dauphine.

I was curious why a talented cyclist would agree to play such a role. "It is an apprenticeship—you have to learn the business," Hugo Peña said. "If you get respect, work well, and are good, you move up." Armstrong himself worked as a *domestique* when he was starting out. He told me that he finds the system reassuring. [Johan] Bruyneel, who was a successful professional, and won two stages in the Tour, agreed. "What does a man gain from riding for himself and coming in fiftieth?" he said. "If you see your job as helping your team win, you will get more out of that than simply riding and losing. It's fun to be part of a winning team." And it is also profitable; even a journeyman cyclist can make a hundred thousand dollars a year. . . . Still, there comes a point when a talented cyclist no longer wants to occupy a supporting role and tries to establish himself as a potential leader.[24]

It was not easy for Armstrong to accept this etiquette of international cycling. As he admits, "I raced with no respect. Absolutely none. I paraded, mouthed off, shoved my fists in the air. I never backed down. The journalists loved me; I was different, I made good copy, I was colorful. But I was making enemies."[25]

These enemies would do whatever they could to impede Armstrong's progress. At various times they would cut him off, isolate him from the leaders, increase their pace to make him work harder, elbow him while jockeying for position, and so on. His teammates finally impressed upon him the need to change his tactics. His lack of maturity was hurting not only himself, but his team as well.

## An Unusual Form of Insult

It was not easy for Armstrong to change. Talk did not have as much of an effect on him as did the actions of Moreno Argentin, a veteran cyclist and former world champion. Shortly after Armstrong turned pro, he faced Argentin in the Tour of the Mediterranean, a major race in France. The newcomer felt Argentin insulted him during the race when he accidentally called him by the name of another rider. Armstrong cursed the veteran rider, drawing his wrath.

A few days later the two men met again in the Trophée Laigueglia, a one-day classic race in Italy. Although Argentin was the favorite, Armstrong challenged him for the lead along with two other riders. With the finish line in sight, Armstrong edged ahead of Argentin. About 5 yards (4.6m) from the finish line, however, the Italian braked, allowing the other two riders to finish second and third. By coming in fourth, Argentin finished out of the medals. In effect, he was showing Armstrong he did not want to stand beside him on the winner's podium, an unusual insult to say the least—and an effective one. Armstrong began to make an effort to change his ways, and the two men later became good friends.

## Strategy and Tactics

Although Armstrong's racing etiquette began to improve, his re-sults continued to be inconsistent. His physical strength helped him make several strong showings, but at other times he did not even finish among the top twenty riders. He could not understand why he was not winning, despite being stronger than almost all his opponents.

Eventually the words of his coaches and teammates began to sink in. Armstrong began to understand the tactics involved in racing on various courses, at various distances, and over various terrain. Gradually he was showing signs of maturing.

In the summer of 1993, Thrift Drugs put up a bonus of $1 million to anyone who could win the three races comprising the U.S. Triple Crown of Cycling. The races were the one-day Thrift Drug Classic in Pittsburgh, the six-day K-Mart Classic in West Virginia, and the one-day CoreStates/U.S. Pro Championships in Philadelphia. For one rider to win all three was a long shot. It would require someone to be a sprinter, a climber, and a stage racer. Such a combination was rare.

Armstrong set the Triple Crown as his goal. He won the first two races, setting the stage for a dramatic 156-mile (251km) run through Philadelphia. Competing against 119 riders, Armstrong rode an almost perfect race. He paced himself over most of the course, then charged to victory over the final twenty miles. (Armstrong did not pocket the $1 million bonus for the win. The team decided on a $600,000 single payment, rather than accepting $50,000 a year for twenty years. After $210,000 was taken by the Internal Revenue Service, the rest was divided among the team members. Armstrong's share was approximately $30,000.)

## A Dreamlike Summer

Armstrong followed up his win with several other victories. He raced in the Tour de France but was realistic in his expectations. "I'm here to learn, really," he told one interviewer. "I don't expect anything.

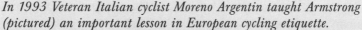

*In 1993 Veteran Italian cyclist Moreno Argentin taught Armstrong (pictured) an important lesson in European cycling etiquette.*

I don't expect to win a stage, I don't expect to take a jersey."[26] Armstrong did better than he had hoped he would. At age twenty-one, he became the youngest rider ever to win one of the Tour's stages. Although Armstrong was not yet ready to compete for the Tour title and dropped out after the twelfth stage, in ninety-seventh place, the experience was invaluable. Said Motorola rider Sean Yates, "He's won a stage, and how many people have done that? It's been a bit of an eye-opener for him. He's learned that it's a bloody hard race. But he learns quickly. He's got respect at the right times, and he fears no one."[27]

Ochowicz was certain Armstrong was now ready to defeat the best racers in the world in the World Championships. He continued to remind him to be patient. "The only thing you have to do is wait," he said. "Just *wait*. Two or three laps is soon enough. Anything earlier and you'll waste your chance to win. But after that, you can attack as many times as you want."[28]

## A Language All Its Own

Cycling has its own language. Many terms and phrases that are unfamiliar to the average person are commonplace at cycling competitions. Some likely to be heard at a race include the following:

**bonk:** When a rider completely runs out of energy; in marathon running it is known as "hitting the wall."

*domestique:* A rider who sacrifices individual honors for himself so that the team leader has a chance to win.

**drafting:** Riding in the air pocket close behind another rider in order to conserve energy. The lead rider expends as much as 30 percent more energy than the drafting rider.

**echelon:** Also known as a "pace line," a line of riders who take turns at the lead. It is staggered so that each rider gets maximum protection from the wind.

**hook:** When a rider uses the rear wheel to hit the wheel of the rider behind him or her. It may be intentional or accidental.

**peloton:** The main pack of riders.

**pull:** To take a turn at the front and break the wind for the other riders in the pack.

**wheel sucker:** A derogatory term for a rider who sits in a drafting position to conserve energy and never takes a pull at the front.

## A Winning Combination

Prior to the race, Armstrong called his mother and asked her to fly out to stay with him. She took time off from work and joined him in Oslo, Norway. In the days leading up to the race, Linda did his laundry, cooked for him, and made sure he got his rest. She helped him put everything else out of his mind, leaving him to concentrate solely on the race.

The day of the race arrived, and weather conditions could not have been worse for cycling. Torrential rains soaked the roads, making the course treacherous. One small mistake and a rider could easily be thrown from his bike. Armstrong crashed two times over the 18.4-kilometer (11.4-mile) course, but he managed to remain in contention. On the second-to-last climb, he finally made his move. He charged up the hill and started to pull away from the other riders. Using every last ounce of energy, he made it through the climbs safely and into the lead. As he neared the finish line, he pumped his arms in the air in victory. He crossed the line, dismounted from his bike, and ran over to his mother. They hugged and both began to cry as Armstrong yelled, "We did it! We did it!" [29]

Following the postrace celebration, Armstrong was approached by a royal escort who informed him that King Harald of Norway wanted to meet him. As Linda later related:

> I told him to go ahead; I'll wait. But he refused to go ahead without me.
>
> We passed through four security checkpoints and each time they told me that I couldn't come with him. But he stayed firm. "I want to experience this with you," he said.
>
> We met the king and that was very nice, but I could tell that Lance was still thinking about the race and how far we had come. [30]

## Growing as a Cyclist

The next few years were a learning period for Armstrong, with improvement coming in small increments rather than in large leaps. The Olympic Training Center in Colorado Springs tested Armstrong following his victory in the Worlds. Researchers there poked, prodded, and evaluated Armstrong to find his various physical thresholds and limits. He began to develop an appreciation for the technical aspects of cycling—the things that would ultimately help him become the best rider possible.

Paying attention to details, such as adjusting his seating position and optimizing his pedal cadence, resulted in several impressive performances. In 1994 Armstrong finished second in Liège-Bastogne-Liège in France (the oldest race in cycling), second in San Sebastián, and second in the Tour DuPont in the eastern United States.

Despite his continued growth as a cyclist, Armstrong was not making as much progress as he had hoped. Some other riders seemed to have improved even more. Samuel Abt relates the bicyclist's thoughts:

> "It seems to be much more difficult this year for some reason," he continued. "There's a lot of guys that go much faster this year. I'm just as fit and feel as good as I did last year, but my strength within the peloton has sort of gone down. A lot of riders are stronger." He did not know it then, but 1994 is now generally regarded as the beginning of the era of EPO, the illegal artificial hormone that enhances performance by multiplying the red blood corpuscles that carry oxygen to exhausted muscles. Italian teams especially are now believed to have started to use the drug that year. Although he knew none of this specifically, Armstrong suspected something.
>
> "It's harder to race this year, cycling is harder now," he said. "In a year, I tell you, man. I hate to point fingers, and I'm not going to do that, but there are a lot of guys who are a lot better and a lot faster than last year." [31]

## A Tragic Tour

By the end of 1994, Armstrong had earned a reputation as a single-day racer. His attacking style and high threshold for pain were well suited to the one-day affairs. He still did not have the endurance, however, to succeed in longer competitions. It was not until 1995 that he finished the Tour de France for the first time.

*Armstrong leads a group of riders up a climb during the 1994 Tour DuPont, a grueling multistage race. Armstrong went on to finish second overall that year.*

The 1995 Tour was marked by tragedy, particularly for Armstrong and his Motorola teammates. One cyclist, 1992 Olympic champion Fabio Casartelli, was killed in a chain-reaction accident that occurred on a high-speed descent in the Tour's fifteenth stage. Casartelli was thrown from his bike and hit the back of his head against a curb. Not wearing a helmet, he suffered fatal injuries to his skull and neck.

Armstrong later learned that Casartelli had set two goals for the Tour: to finish the race and to win the stage into Limoges. Armstrong became determined to finish the race himself and to win the stage into Limoges for Casartelli. He proceeded to do both, winning the eighteenth stage by a full minute.

## Tour de France Fatalities

Fabio Casartelli's tragic death in the 1995 Tour de France was not the first time the race was marked by tragedy. Nearly thirty years earlier, English rider Tom Simpson collapsed from heat exhaustion and died on the ascent of Mount Ventoux. Although his death was officially attributed to heart failure, an autopsy revealed traces of amphetamines in his body. The drugs were also found on his jersey. Simpson's death prompted the sport to begin a drug-testing program. There is a memorial to him on the way up the climb, as there is to Casartelli on the Col de Portet d'Aspet, where he suffered his fatal accident.

Spanish rider Francisco Cepeda was the first rider to die during the race. He succumbed after plunging down a ravine on the Col du Galibier in the French Alps during the 1935 Tour. Two other Tour-related deaths occurred in 1957 when radio reporter Alex Virot and his motorcyclist driver, René Wagner, fell into a ravine during the Barcelona-Ax-les-Thermes stage while covering the event.

*Italian cyclist Fabio Casartelli celebrates his gold medal win in the 1992 Olympic road race in Barcelona.*

The 1995 Tour had a profound effect on Armstrong. As he wrote:

> There were no shortcuts, I realized. It took years of racing to build up the mind and body and character, until a rider had logged hundreds of races and thousands of miles of road. I wouldn't be able to win a Tour de France until I had enough iron in my legs, and lungs, and brain, and heart. Until I was a man. Fabio had been a man. I was still trying to get there. [32]

The following year, the road to becoming a man would be paved with yet another obstacle. This one would dwarf all the rest.

# Chapter 3

# Cancer

By 1996 ARMSTRONG was beginning to show signs of fulfilling his potential. That spring he became the first American ever to win Belgium's grueling Fleche-Wallone. He finished second in the classic Liège-Bastogne-Liège, then followed with a win in the twelve-day-long Tour DuPont through the mountains of Carolina. He was runner-up in five other races and seemed on the verge of breaking into the top five in the international rankings.

Despite his successes, however, something was not quite right. Armstrong was more tired than usual when he finished races, and he had aches and pains where he never had them before. He experienced soreness in his nipples and noticed a swelling in his right testicle. Because he was riding well, however, and had no other symptoms, such as loss of appetite or weight loss, he attributed these aches to nothing more than the side effects associated with cycling. "The only thing I had," he later remembered, "was an enlarged testicle. It didn't hurt, didn't affect me in any way, it was just there." [33]

Shortly after his twenty-fifth birthday that September, Armstrong had some friends over to a party at his newly-built house. He had recently signed a new $2.5-million contract with the French racing team Cofidis. Later that night, Armstrong got a headache that would not go away. He finally got to sleep, and the headache was gone when he woke up the next morning. His vision, however, was a little blurry.

A couple days later he suffered a severe coughing attack that left a metallic taste in his mouth. Retreating to his bathroom, he began coughing up blood into the sink. Frightened, Armstrong called Rick Parker, a physician and friend who lived nearby. Parker came over to examine him and suggested he might have cracked one of his sinuses. Armstrong accepted the explanation until his testicle became even more swollen and painful a few days later. Parker insisted he get checked out by Jim Reeves, a prominent area urologist (a doctor who specializes in diseases of the urinary tract).

Reeves thought the swelling and soreness might simply be due to a torsion (twisting) of the testicle, but he asked Armstrong to undergo an ultrasound test just to be safe. This test involves using high-frequency sound waves and a computer to create images of blood vessels, tissues, and organs in order to assess the blood flow through the body. Reeves then asked for a chest X-ray, and Armstrong knew something was wrong. When he and Parker went to Reeves's office for the results, they received devastating news. "This is a serious situation," Reeves told them. "It looks like testicular cancer with large metastasis to the lungs."[34] In nonmedical terms, this meant he had a rare form of an often-fatal disease, and it had spread to other parts of his body. Armstrong was incredulous. "I'm 25 years old," he said. "I'm one of the best in my sport—why would I have cancer? I had lots of tests all through my career, physical tests, blood tests, and they never picked this up."[35]

*Armstrong adjusts his helmet during the 1996 Tour DuPont. Later that year, he was diagnosed with testicular cancer.*

## Would He Ever Race Again?

Cancer is a malignant growth or tumor that is caused by abnormal and uncontrolled cell division. It can spread to other parts of the body. Testicular cancer is a fairly rare disease, with approximately seven thousand new cases annually in the United States. It usually strikes men between the ages of eighteen and twenty-five. With new advances in the field of medicine, the prognosis (chance for recovery) is good when it is caught in the early stages. As Parker told Armstrong, "There's been so much improvement in the treatment of cancer. It's curable. Whatever it takes, we'll get it whipped. We'll get it done." [36] Reeves scheduled him for surgery to have the testicle removed the next morning.

Armstrong's first worry was that he would never race again. It was not until later that fear really hit him, and he realized that he could not only lose his career, but also his life. His mother and his friends rallied around him to offer encouragement.

Armstrong decided the first step in fighting his disease was to find out everything he could about it. With the help of his friend Bart Knaggs, he downloaded material on testicular cancer off the Internet. He learned that oncologists (doctors who specialize in the treatment of cancer) broke the disease down into three categories, or stages. In the first—and least advanced—the cancer is confined to the testicles. The prognosis for patients in this stage is excellent. In stage two, the cancer has spread to the abdominal lymph nodes (structures in the body that produce white blood cells and filter bacteria and cancer cells that might travel through the body). In stage three—the most advanced stage—the cancer has spread to vital organs such as the lungs. At each stage, the chances for recovery are reduced. Despite Reeves's belief that the disease had already spread to his lungs, Armstrong still held out hope that his cancer was in the first stage.

## More Bad News

The surgery the following morning lasted three hours, from beginning through recovery. The next day, as he lay resting in his room, Armstrong received the initial results of the reports and blood tests. The news was worse than he had expected. The cancer appeared to be spreading rapidly. Some had been discovered

## Hope for the Future

Until 1970 a diagnosis of testicular cancer usually carried a death sentence. Approximately 90 percent of those diagnosed died of the disease. The decade of the 1970s, however, brought with it a drastic change with the introduction of the drug cisplatin. When used together with other chemotherapy drugs (and appropriate surgery), cisplatin increased the cure rate to 80 percent.

As Craig Nichols notes on the Testicular Cancer Resource Center Web site, however, "Why the combination works so well in this disease and hardly at all in others is unknown." According to Nichols, it is believed that the drugs kill the tumor cells by disrupting their ability to divide and reproduce. In some way they also cause the death rate of the cells to accelerate.

The successful use of cisplatin has allowed doctors to decrease the use of other more potentially dangerous treatments. Surgeries have become less drastic, and surveillance, or watchful waiting, has become an option. This is possible because doctors are more confident they can cure any recurrence as long as the cancer is caught early.

in his abdomen. The three different forms of cancer in his body included chariocarcinoma, an aggressive type carried through the blood that is very hard to stop.

Armstrong's doctors told him he would begin chemotherapy—treatment involving the administration of chemicals to destroy cancer cells—the following week. To begin treatments, doctors needed to implant a catheter, a thin plastic tube used to either add or remove fluid, in his chest. Treatments would last three months. On top of this, he was told that chemotherapy often leaves patients sterile. Armstrong was advised to have some of his sperm frozen in case he decided he wanted to have children some day. He did so several days later.

By that time Armstrong had received further bad news. Dudley Youman, an Austin-based oncologist, called to tell him that the cancer was progressing at an even more rapid rate than the doctors had originally suspected. His first chemo treatment would have to be sooner than they had planned. With this news Armstrong decided it was time to go public. He held a press conference at which he disclosed his condition. "I'm determined to fight this disease," he concluded. "And I will win."[37] Inwardly, however, Armstrong had some doubts. Abt reported Armstrong's thoughts:

> "From the first moment I learned this, I thought, 'Oh my God, I'm going to die'. I went from being at the top of my game, fourth in World Cup races in Leeds and Zurich, to being told I had cancer. Eventually you get over that. I said, 'Forget the numbers, forget the chances the doctors give you, forget it. We're going to work hard and we're going to win this. I'm not going to die, I'm going to live.' I chose to live, to fight to live.

> "But if you're the biggest, toughest guy out there and saying, 'I'm going to live,' there are cases where you do die. Because cancer does not recognize that. It does not play fair. It's aggressive, it's smart, it's tough, it's relentless, it adapts, it becomes resistant to therapies. If it wants to win, it can win."[38]

*At the time this photo was taken in early 1997, Armstrong had undergone several rounds of chemotherapy and surgery to remove two lesions from his brain.*

## Treatment Begins

The treatment Youman prescribed for Armstrong was standard for testicular cancer patients, a three-drug combination called BEP. The drugs prescribed were very potent. Armstrong was scheduled for treatments administered in a three-week cycle: one week of chemo followed by two weeks off to allow his body to recuperate. Youman estimated his chance of recovery at 60 to 65 percent.

Armstrong was determined to defeat the disease. After he began his treatments, he continued to exercise daily, either walking or riding his bike. In his mind he had convinced himself that if he could ride, he could not be that sick. Luckily the chemo did not cause the nausea and vomiting in him that are common with most new patients.

## The Low Point

After going public with his disease, Armstrong received an outpouring of letters and get-well cards from people around the country. One letter was from Steven Wolff of Vanderbilt University's medical center. Wolff was an avid cycling fan and offered to help in any way he could.

The standard three-drug cocktail Armstrong began to take in his chemotherapy regimen included bleomycin, a drug that is extremely toxic to the liver and lungs. As a cycling fan, Wolff was aware of the importance of strong lungs to an athlete. "You should note," said Wolff after speaking to Armstrong, "that there are equally effective chemotherapy treatments that could minimize possible side effects to not compromise your racing capabilities." [39] The suggestion that some other combination of drugs might be effective and not permanently damage his lungs gave Armstrong hope he might be able to race again someday.

Wolff also suggested that Armstrong contact Lawrence Einhorn, one of the landmark researchers in the treatment of testicular cancer. Einhorn's work at the Indiana University Medical Center in Indianapolis had led to the use of a platinum compound called cisplatin that dramatically changed the prognosis for testicular cancer patients. Prior to his work, testicular cancer was almost always a fatal disease.

In the course of their conversation, Wolff asked Armstrong what his human chorionic gonadotropin (HCG) level was. HCG is an endocrine protein that is usually not present in healthy males, but it is sometimes found in testicular tumors. A count of 100 is considered high; Armstrong's count was 109,000. To Wolff this indicated that the protein was coming from someplace other than just the tumors in his abdomen. He suggested Armstrong consult with the doctors at the Indiana University Medical Center and two other cancer centers in Houston and New York.

Two days later doctors evaluated Armstrong's brain with an MRI (magnetic resonance imaging) machine, a device that produces detailed images from inside the body. The results of the scan were not promising. The tests revealed two growths on his brain. At this point, doctors said, Armstrong's chances of survival were poor, close to 20 percent.

## New Hope

The doctors at the medical center in Houston did not offer Armstrong much more encouragement. They wanted him to begin treatment immediately and suggested an even more caustic regimen of drugs. Because of the effects of the bleomycin, they too offered little hope that he would ever be able to race again. When he mentioned this to Wolff, his friend again suggested he visit the Indiana University Medical Center.

At Indiana, Armstrong spoke with Einhorn's associate, Craig Nichols, and neurosurgeon Scott Shapiro. After reviewing Armstrong's medical records, the two doctors gave Armstrong a more encouraging view. They thought he had a 50-50 chance of survival.

Nichols also held out hope that Armstrong might someday race again. In order to do this, he wanted to change Armstrong's chemo combination to one called VIP—a combination of drugs without bleomycin. This mixture would be more painful in the short run, causing more nausea and vomiting, but it would be less harmful in the long run. Said Armstrong, "The side effects of bleomycin could potentially prohibit me from ever racing again because of insufficient lung capacity. So we switched off that to preserve my career. For them to feel comfortable enough to switch me off one drug when we were having success, and for them to already consider thinking about my career, I thought was good."[40] Nichols suggested three cycles of VIP.

Nichols also recommended surgery for the removal of the brain tumors rather than the standard radiation treatment in which cancer cells are destroyed by exposure to radiation from a radioactive substance. This would be less likely to cause long-term prob-

## Athletes and Cancer

Lance Armstrong is arguably the most famous athlete struck by cancer in the middle of his career, but he is not the only one. With the aid of new advances in the field of medicine, however, cancer is no longer a death sentence.

In baseball, Houston pitcher Jim Umbricht lost his battle with cancer in 1964 at the age of thirty-three. The following year, twenty-five-year-old Angels hurler Dick Wantz died following brain surgery for cancer. In more recent years, all-star first baseman Andres Galarraga sat out the 1999 season after being diagnosed with non-Hodgkin's lymphoma, but he made a full recovery and returned to the major leagues in 2000.

Hockey superstar Mario Lemieux was diagnosed with Hodgkin's disease—cancer of the lymphatic system—in 1993. He bounced back to play again in the National Hockey League, as did twenty-six-year-old Canadiens captain Saku Koivu, who was afflicted with Burkitt's lymphoma in 2001.

*In 1993 hockey superstar Mario Lemieux was diagnosed with Hodgkin's disease.*

Perhaps the most widely publicized athlete to have been struck down by cancer was Chicago Bears running back Brian Piccolo. Piccolo died of embryonal cell carcinoma in 1970 at the age of twenty-six. His story was recounted in the television movie *Brian's Song*. After his death, the Brian Piccolo Cancer Research Fund was established. Thanks in part to money raised in his name, embryonal cell carcinoma is now almost completely curable.

lems with the central nervous system. Because the lesions appeared to be on the surface of the brain rather than internal, Shapiro did not foresee any problems with surgery.

After talking things over with his family and friends, Armstrong reached a decision. He would continue his treatment at the Indiana University Medical Center. At the suggestion of Nichols, Armstrong took some time off to recuperate from his BEP treatment. A week later he returned to Indianapolis.

## Confronting Mortality

Faced with a serious operation, Armstrong began to examine his personal beliefs more carefully. For the first time in his life, he spent a good deal of time thinking about death:

> The night before brain surgery, I thought about death. I searched out my larger values, and I asked myself, if I was going to die, did I want to do it fighting and clawing or in peaceful surrender? . . .
>
> I asked myself what I believed. I had never prayed a lot. I hoped hard, I wished hard, but I didn't pray. I had developed a certain distrust of organized religion growing up, but I felt I had the capacity to be a spiritual person, and to hold some fervent beliefs. Quite simply, I believed I had a responsibility to be a good person, and that meant fair, honest, hardworking, and honorable. If I did that, if I was good to my family, true to my friends, if I gave back to my community or to some cause, if I wasn't a liar, a cheat, or a thief, then I believed that should be enough. . . .
>
> I believed, too, in the doctors and the medicine and the surgeries—I believed in that, I believed in them. . . .
>
> To continue believing in yourself, believing in the doctors, believing in the treatment, believing in whatever I chose to believe in, that was the most important thing, I decided. It had to be.[41]

## Surgery

On October 25, 1996, doctors removed two lesions from Armstrong's brain during surgery that lasted nearly six hours. The results were

*Before undergoing brain surgery in October 1996, Armstrong spent a good deal of time contemplating his own mortality.*

the best possible. The cancerous cells from the lesions were necrotic, or dead, tissue. Although doctors could not tell what had killed the cells, they knew that the cancer was not spreading.

Within days after the surgery, Armstrong resumed his chemotherapy treatments. This stage was critical. Although the surgery had been a success, the chemo had to prevent the disease from spreading if Armstrong were to survive. "It used to be when I woke up every morning, I knew I was going to wake up," he said. "It was so normal I took it for granted and now I never know. We're not promised anything. We're not promised tomorrow."[42]

# Chapter 4

# The Road Back

FIGHTING CANCER TOOK a severe toll on Armstrong, physically and mentally. It also threatened him financially. Armstrong's surgeries, chemo treatments, and hospital stay cost a significant amount of money. He had recently signed a contract with a new sponsor, Cofidis, and his medical insurance with Motorola had expired. Because the cancer was considered a preexisting medical condition, the Cofidis group insurance plan was not obliged to cover it. Armstrong was told he would have to pay the bill himself.

Faced with this hefty financial expense, Armstrong received some good news from Oakley, a manufacturer of sunglasses and another of his sponsors. After being told of Armstrong's situation, Oakley chief executive officer Mike Parnell said he would take care of the matter. Parnell called Oakley's medical provider and informed the insurer that his entire firm would take its business elsewhere if the insurer did not cover Armstrong's medical bills. Not wanting to take a chance on losing a large account, the provider agreed.

## Side Effects

With the worry of medical bills no longer hanging over him, Armstrong was able to focus exclusively on getting better. This was no small task. The chemo treatments were debilitating. At first they were bearable, but soon the chemicals coursing through his body caused pain, nausea, and vomiting. Armstrong coughed continuously, bringing up clumps of tarlike matter from his lungs.

As the weeks went by, the cumulative effect of the drugs made him constantly sleepy. When he was not on chemo, he was connected to an intravenous (IV) drip of chemicals to protect his immune system from the effects of the drugs. Armstrong described his feelings:

> I felt like my veins were being scoured out. The medical explanation for the sensation I experienced was myelo-suppression, the most frequent and severe side effect of chemotherapy, which is the inhibition of red blood cell production and maturation. . . .
>
> Chemo doesn't just kill cancer—it kills healthy cells, too. It attacked my bone marrow, my muscle, my teeth, and the linings of my throat and stomach, and left me open to all kinds of infections. My gums bled. I got sores in my mouth. And of course I lost my appetite, which was a potentially serious problem. Without enough protein, I wouldn't be able to rebuild tissue after chemo had eaten through my skin, my hair, and my fingernails. [43]

*Fighting cancer weakened Armstrong both physically and mentally, but he was resolved to beat the disease at all costs.*

## Staying Focused

The chemo treatments took a toll on Armstrong's body, but he refused to give up. With the help and encouragement of his nurse, LaTrice Haney, he remained focused on defeating the disease despite the chemo burns on his skin, the burning sensation when he urinated, and the other assorted aches and pains caused by the chemicals in his body.

The Cofidis racing organization's reaction to Armstrong's predicament added to his misery. Publicly Cofidis had pledged to stand by Armstrong as he battled his illness. Privately it reneged. While Armstrong was in the hospital, Cofidis director Alain Bondue told Armstrong that the company would be forced to renegotiate his contract. Cofidis eventually paid less than a third of the $2.5-million contract and insisted on an out clause, allowing the company to cancel the agreement without penalty for the following year. It was obvious the sponsor did not think Armstrong would ever race again.

## Turning the Corner

In less than a month of treatment, Armstrong's body began to respond. His HCG number dropped from more than 90,000 to less

*Wearing a shirt with the Cofidis logo, Armstrong (right) talks with close friend George Hincapie at the 1997 Tour de France. Later that year, Cofidis reneged on Armstrong's contract.*

than 10,000. When his HCG number finally fell below 100, he knew the toughest part was over. Armstrong began to feel he was winning the battle against the disease. Now he believed that all he had to do was get back into shape.

Armstrong's lack of strength made it difficult for him to do much physical activity. While back home in Texas between chemo treatments, he tried to ride his bike despite Nichols's admonition to take it easy.

Because the chemo robbed his body of healthy blood cells, Armstrong's hemoglobin count was low. Hemoglobin is a substance contained within red blood cells that carries oxygen through the bloodstream to the different parts of the body. A lack of oxygen ensured that he would not be able to exert himself for long before becoming tired. Although he was not able to ride for long periods, the exercise did have a positive effect on him mentally. He rode for the sheer pleasure of riding; it helped him get away from his problems. "[His recovery] almost defies reality," said Carmichael. "He's making the doctors look like heroes. They love him." [44]

The pressure stemming from the negotiations with Cofidis gave Armstrong an additional reason to continue to ride. He wanted to show the sponsor that he could make it all the way back from cancer, knowing the company doubted he would ever race again. It took Haney to talk some sense into him, reminding him that his body needed time to rest and recuperate.

## The End of the Road

Armstrong had his last chemo treatment on December 13, 1996. The catheter was finally removed from his body after four long months. He was not, however, finished with cancer. As Nichols explained, the last chemo treatment did not necessarily remove the last remnants of the disease from his body. He would have to undergo monthly blood tests and checkups before he could be certain that the cancer had been beaten.

Although his blood markers were still slightly above normal, Nichols was confident they would continue to drop. (Blood markers are components of the blood that are associated with a particular condition or disease.) At the same time, however, the disease could still return. If it was going to do so, according to most doctors, it would be within the next year.

## Continuing the Fight

Through his months of treatment, Armstrong had developed a deep feeling of companionship with other cancer patients. He shared experiences with them and tried to give them hope in their battles against the disease. It seemed to help them knowing that a world-class athlete was going through the same things they were.

With the encouragement of Nichols, Armstrong decided to form an organization to help cancer patients. He was not sure yet how his organization would help, but he knew it was something he had to create. And so the Lance Armstrong Foundation was born.

The foundation's first activity was a charity bicycle race called the Ride for the Roses. Approximately one month after his last chemo treatment, Armstrong held a press conference to announce the launching of the foundation and the Ride for the Roses. While there he met a young, blonde-haired woman named Kristin Richard, an account executive for a public relations firm that was helping to promote the event. Over the next couple of months, Armstrong got to know "Kik" (as she was called) better and better as they worked closely together on the foundation.

The Ride for the Roses was held in March 1997 and was a huge success. After the race was over, Armstrong and Richard continued to stay in contact. It was obvious that their relationship was growing into something more than just a friendship.

## Thoughts of a Comeback

As Armstrong continued to build his strength, he decided he would at least make one attempt to return to racing. He began training seriously that spring, but he still tired fairly quickly. When Nichols suggested he take the rest of the year off to give his immune system a chance to rebound from the harsh chemo regimen, Armstrong agreed.

In some ways, Armstrong found recovering from cancer harder than having it. It was difficult for him to just rest and let his body heal. He played a lot of golf and spent more and more time around his house. The time away from racing caused him to

## Ride for the Roses Weekend

The original 1997 Ride for the Roses has grown by leaps and bounds in succeeding years. It is now part of the Run for the Roses Weekend held in Austin, Texas, each October. The 2004 weekend was composed of several events, including the PowerBar Health & Sports Expo, which featured cancer screening services, information on cancer awareness, sports gear and apparel, and new product demonstrations; the LiveStrong Kids event, consisting of a 1-mile (1.6km) walk followed by other kid-friendly activities; the Ride for the Roses, where thousands of participants joined Lance Armstrong and other celebrities for a ride through the Austin Hill country to bring awareness for cancer survivorship; and a post-ride party. The 2004 weekend raised $5.5 million for the Lance Armstrong Foundation.

*Cyclists compete in the 2001 Ride for the Roses. All money raised from the annual event goes to the Lance Armstrong Foundation.*

have second thoughts about his comeback. For one of the few times in his life, he considered giving up.

Armstrong's feelings did not change until he and Richard began seeing each other on a more serious basis. He admired her toughness, independence, and willingness to say what was on her mind. By the end of the summer, the pair had declared their love for one another.

Richard flew to Indianapolis with Armstrong for his monthly checkups. The reports continued to be positive, with the X-rays showing no recurrence of the cancer and the blood tests remaining normal. His chances for suffering a relapse were shrinking with every passing day. As the one-year anniversary of the diagnosis approached, Carmichael began to encourage Armstrong to make another attempt at racing. Armstrong finally decided to try a comeback.

## A New Team

When Armstrong notified Cofidis officials that he was planning a comeback, they suggested he come to France to meet with them. Once there they delivered disheartening news. "We want to thank you for coming here," said Cofidis executive officer François Migraine, "but we want you to know that we're going to exercise our right to terminate [your] contract. We need to go in a

*Armstrong rides alongside the United States Postal Service team car at the 2003 Tour de France. After Cofidis dropped him, Armstrong signed with the USPS cycling team.*

different direction."[45] Cofidis eventually called back to offer him a contract for $180,000, a fraction of his previous contract.

Feeling betrayed by the offer, Armstrong and his agent, Bill Stapleton, traveled to California for the Interbike Expo. He refused the lowball offer and held a press conference to announce his comeback and the termination of his contract by Cofidis. He expected to receive offers from other racing teams, but none was forthcoming. No European team would agree to Armstrong's asking price of $500,000. "I've offered myself up for the league minimum, and I can't even get that," said Armstrong. "I can't get people to call me back. Now I know what it feels like to be shunned."[46]

The U.S. Postal Service team, a new American-funded and -sponsored organization, eventually contacted Stapleton. It, too, offered just a low base salary. Thomas Weisel, the team's chief investor, however, was an old friend of Armstrong's as the former owner of the Subaru-Montgomery team for which he had raced. When Armstrong and Stapleton approached Weisel personally, he agreed to give Armstrong a $215,000 base salary with incentives that could earn him substantial bonus money. "It wasn't much compared with what I had been making," recalled Armstrong. "But Thom had stacked it with incentive bonuses based on performances. That gave me a chance to ride again on a team."[47]

Armstrong later confided to a friend, "I guess I can react one of two ways. I can say, 'Hey, listen, I've raced bikes for five or six years, I've been successful and just, well, move on.' Or, I can say, 'I'm [angry] and I'm going to find a ride somewhere and make everybody look like fools.'"[48]

Having made his decision, Armstrong returned to Austin to see Richard. He told her about his plans to return to racing in Europe in January and that he wanted her with him. Armstrong proposed marriage, and Richard accepted. The couple planned their wedding for May 1998.

## A Disappointing Return

Armstrong and Richard moved to France in January 1998 and took an apartment in Cap Ferrat, halfway between Nice and Monaco. Although Armstrong's body was coming back physically, he still had doubts about his ability to be as good as he once

## A Championship Team Evolves

The U.S. Postal Service team can trace its roots back to 1988. That year, former U.S. National Team coach Eddie Borysewicz formed an amateur team sponsored by Sunkyong, a Korean electronics firm. (The sponsor pays the team's operating expenses in return for publicity and marketing benefits.) The team only lasted for a year, but it laid the groundwork for a new squad sponsored by Montgomery Securities. Montgomery eventually joined forces with Subaru automobiles. This was the team Lance Armstrong joined as an amateur in 1990.

Subaru-Montgomery eventually expanded its role into overseas competition, with an eye toward a spot in the Tour de France. After three years, however, the team did not achieve that goal and Subaru decided to end its sponsorship. The U.S. Postal Service became the squad's title sponsor for the 1996 season. The team eventually signed up a group of young American and seasoned European riders.

The next year, U.S. Postal placed a team in the Tour for the first time. The squad finished eighth overall while winning two stages. By the end of the 1997 season, it made the move that assured its future success by signing Armstrong.

was. He resented the fact that he was making only a fraction of his old salary, and he took out his frustrations on those around him.

Armstrong's attitude did not improve when he finished fourteenth in his first race back, a five-day trek through Spain called the Ruta del Sol. Two weeks later he finished in nineteenth place in the Prologue (a time-trial competition that determines who rides at the front of the peloton) at Paris-Nice. The next day he became further demoralized by his poor performance in the cold, wet weather. In the middle of the race, he pulled over to the side of the road, took off his number, and quit.

Armstrong returned home and told Richard of his decision. "I don't know how much time I have left," he said, "but I don't want to spend it cycling. I hate it. I hate the conditions. I hate being away from you. I hate this lifestyle over here. I don't want to be in Europe. I proved myself in Ruta del Sol, I showed that I could come back and do it. I have nothing left to prove to myself, or to the cancer community, so that's it."[49]

The couple returned to the United States, but Stapleton convinced Armstrong to hold off on issuing a formal announcement of his retirement. Stapleton suggested he ride one farewell race back home, possibly the national championships in June. Armstrong agreed to wait until at least the Ride for the Roses in May.

## A Wake-up Call

In the weeks following his return home, Armstrong did nothing but play golf and lie around the house. Determined to never deprive himself of anything ever again, he broke every rule of his training diet. He drank beer, ate loads of Tex-Mex food, and lazed around the house. Perhaps surprisingly, he was not happy. He had spent a good part of his life on a bike and did not know how to handle being away from it.

Richard was also struggling with Armstrong's retirement. She finally confronted him one afternoon as he was heading out to the golf course.

> "You need to decide something," she told him. "You need to decide if you are going to retire for real, and be a golf-playing, beer-drinking, Mexican-food-eating slob. If you are,

> that's fine. I love you, and I'll marry you anyway. But I just need to know, so I can get myself to-gether and go back on the street, and get a job to support your golfing. Just tell me.
>
> "But if you're not go-ing to retire, then you need to stop eating and drinking like this and being a bum, and

*Kristin Richard and Armstrong wed in May 1998, shortly after Armstrong decided not to retire from professional cycling.*

you need to figure it out, because you are deciding by not deciding, and that is so un-Lance. It is just not you. And I'm not quite sure who you are right now. I love you anyway, but you need to figure something out."[50]

Stapleton, Carmichael, and Ochowicz also urged him to reconsider his decision to retire. Carmichael was able to convince him to train for the second Ride for the Roses. He had to get away from Austin, however, to immerse himself in the training regimen. Armstrong decided to go to the small town of Boone, North Carolina, where he had won the Tour DuPont in 1995 and 1996.

Under Carmichael's watchful eye, Armstrong began to return to racing form. Carmichael had said, "My gut tells me Lance is going to come back to peak faster than any of us might have thought."[51] Armstrong trained as if determined to make his friend's prediction come true. He rode every day, regardless of weather and road conditions. At night the two old friends would reminisce, telling stories and laughing about days gone by. When Armstrong called Richard, she could sense a difference in his attitude. He was having fun again, enjoying the routine and rigors of training. By the time his training period was over, Armstrong had been revitalized. He was a bike racer once again. "That was just plain old-fashioned riding bikes," he recalled. "That's all we really went to do—call it training, call it bike riding, whatever. We just had a good time, neat company for six hours a day, which isn't easy to do. And it was raining every day. So I figured that if I could do that, ride six hours a day in the rain, then I must want to do it. That's all."[52]

On May 9, 1998, following his training jaunt to Boone, the couple married in Santa Barbara, California. After a brief honeymoon on the beach, they returned to Austin for the second annual Ride for the Roses.

# Chapter 5

# The 1999 Tour de France

ARMSTRONG'S OFFICIAL RETURN to cycling came in June 1998, just a month after his wedding. His fourth-place finish at the U.S. Pro Championships helped buoy his spirits and reassure him he had made the right decision to return to the sport he loved.

The next step in his comeback was a return to international competition. He entered—and won—the Tour of Luxembourg. Although the four-day race is not considered an especially prestigious event, Armstrong considered it a very important step in his comeback. "In Luxembourg," he said, "I only wanted to finish the race. That was my only motivation. I learned during that time in North Carolina how much racing meant to me."[53] His victory removed any last doubts he harbored about being able to compete at the highest level. He began devoting all his energy to his return to racing. He continued to make steady progress and captured fourth place in another race. Realizing that he was not yet ready for the three-week marathon, he decided to forgo the 1998 Tour de France. Instead his goal became a victory in the 1999 Tour de France.

## Another Step Forward

At the end of September, Armstrong competed in the three-week Vuelta a España (Tour of Spain). Riding more than 2,300 miles (3,701km) in twenty-three days in freezing temperatures, he narrowly missed making the awards podium. Despite not winning, the race was especially meaningful to Armstrong. Prior to his diagnosis, he

*In 1998 Armstrong officially returned to professional cycling. He is shown here in action at that year's World Championships in Belgium.*

had earned his reputation as a one-day racer. His strong finish in the Vuelta made him confident of his ability to compete in races of any length. He was convinced he was a better racer than ever before. As he continued his training, he found he had an even stronger incentive to work toward a successful comeback. He and his wife had planned to start a family right after the New Year in 1999. In February of that year, Kik underwent in vitro fertilization to conceive a child with the sperm Armstrong had frozen before undergoing chemotherapy. Within two weeks, the Armstrongs learned the procedure had worked: She was pregnant.

## The Tour de France

Armstrong's success in the Vuelta a España made him believe he might have a chance to win the Tour de France. Arguably the toughest endurance race in the world, the Tour is a long-distance competition that has been held annually (interrupted only by the two world wars) since 1903, when it was started by the newspaper *L'Auto*. Sixty riders competed in that first race. Only twenty-one finished.

The event quickly captivated the imagination of the nation. Tens of thousands of spectators come out to line the roads and cheer on the riders. The race is composed of around twenty stages, each of which is a one-day race. The total length of the Tour runs between 3,000 and 4,000 kilometers, or more than 2,000 miles. The stages usually run through France, although individual stages have been held in nearby countries over the years.

The Tour begins with a short individual time trial known as the Prologue and finishes with a final, traditional stage ending on the Champs Elysées in Paris. The stages in between include individual time trials, a team time trial, several mountain stages, and other stages over relatively flat terrain. Winners are named for each stage, with the racer with the best overall time declared the Tour champion.

## Preparations

Armstrong had decided to sacrifice his entire 1999 season to prepare for the Tour de France. He skipped several of the early, prestigious races in order to concentrate on those that would get him ready to peak in July. Armstrong passed on many of the one-day, shorter races in which he had made his name. His style was somewhat toned down, no longer as aggressive as it had been in the past. He now paid more attention to techniques that would enable him to succeed in longer events such as the Tour.

Armstrong—together with U.S. Postal team riders Frankie Andreu, Kevin Livingston, Tyler Hamilton, George Hincapie, Christian Vandevelde, Pascal Derame, Jonathan Vaughters, and Peter Meinert-Neilsen—spent a great deal of time training in the Pyrenees, the mountain range that extends along the border between France and Spain. Former Tour rider Bruyneel, the team's director, planned training camps where team members practiced riding the mountainous sections they would face in the Tour.

Although he had won two stages in the past, Armstrong had only finished one Tour. Now, however, his body seemed better suited for such races. In the past, when he had raced at 170 pounds (77kg), his body had been more muscular from his days as a triathlete. Now he weighed just 158 pounds (72kg). This helped him on climbs where extra weight was an impediment. "The less I weigh, the better off I am in the mountains," he said. "Losing 10 pounds is like throwing a barbell away every time I ride uphill."[54]

Armstrong maintained his weight by methodically measuring every bite of food he put into his mouth. He kept careful records of caloric intake so that he knew exactly how much to eat, and how much energy to expend, in order to lose weight when necessary. His meticulousness bore fruit and his climbing ability improved. Armstrong's willingness to punish his body set him apart from other riders. He practiced for hours at a time in all kinds of weather.

## The Prologue

Having prepared himself to the best of his abilities, Armstrong arrived in Paris in June for the preliminaries to the Tour, including drug tests. The riders made last-minute adjustments to their bikes. Armstrong attended to his equipment in the same meticulous way he attended to his body, earning the nickname "Mister Millimeter" from his crew.

With the preliminaries out of the way, the riders gathered for the Prologue. The Prologue was an 8-kilometer (5-mile) time trial in which the racers rode as hard as they could. Those with the fastest times would ride at the front of the peloton.

The course in the Vendée region of western France consisted of a flat 5-kilometer (3.1-mile) stretch, followed by a steep hill and a flat sprint to the finish. The course record for the prologue had been 8:12, set by the great racer Induráin. That record was broken by world champion Abraham Olano, who finished in 8:11. His mark, in turn, was bested by Alexander Zülle's 8:07. When it was Armstrong's turn, he finished in a blazing 8:02 to set a new record and win the yellow jersey, or *maillot jaune,* that is awarded to the leader. Even Armstrong had a hard time believing what he had done.

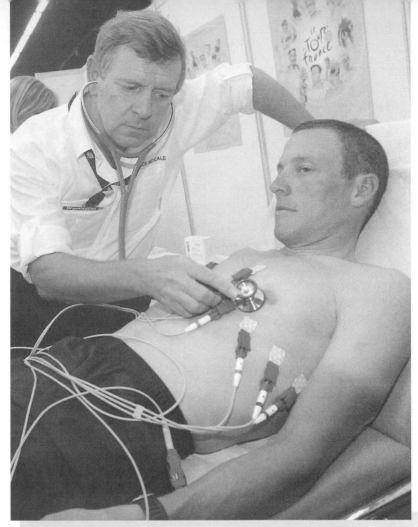

*A doctor monitors Armstrong's heart during the mandatory medical exam all riders undergo before the start of the Tour de France.*

## The Opening Stages

As Stage 1 began in Montaigu on the plains of western France on July 1, Armstrong rode with the honor of being the first American to ride for an American team, on an American bike, to lead the Tour de France. The early stages were over mostly flat terrain that favored the sprinters. Armstrong retained the yellow jersey after the first stage.

During Stage 2—a run from Challans to the military port of Saint-Nazaire—a massive pileup occurred on a section called the Passage du Gois. The passage is a long, narrow road across a tidal marsh. During high tides, water covers the road, making it nearly

## Jerseys of the Tour

At the end of each stage of the Tour de France, various colored jerseys are awarded to the riders. The most prestigious of all is the yellow jersey, or *maillot jaune*. This is awarded to the rider who is the leader in the overall standings. Yellow signifies the color pages used to print *L'Auto*, the cycling newspaper that founded the Tour. The rider wears the jersey during the next stage, making it easier for him to be recognized.

A green jersey (*maillot vert*) is presented to the leader of the points standings, generally one of the top sprinters. Points are awarded, based on the position in which a rider finishes, at the end of each stage. The best climber, or "King of the Mountains," is given a white jersey with red polka dots (*maillot à pois*). Two lesser prizes are the white jersey for the leader in the young riders standings and the red number for the most aggressive rider. Each member of the squad leading in the team standings wears a yellow cap during the next stage.

The jerseys are awarded in a ceremony that is held immediately following a stage. If a rider leads in more than one category, he wears only the most prestigious jersey, with the second-place rider in the lesser category donning the other jersey.

*At the 2004 Tour, Armstrong sports the* maillot jaune *as he shakes hands with Richard Virenque in the polka-dot jersey and Robbie McEwen in the green jersey.*

impassable. Luckily Armstrong and most of his teammates were in the group at the front. They made it through without any mishaps. The second group, however, was not as lucky. Many of the top riders lost significant time in a huge chain-reaction pileup.

Armstrong eventually surrendered the yellow jersey to Mario Cipollini of Italy, who enjoyed a spectacular week with four consecutive stage wins. U.S. Postal's team director, Dan Osipow, explained that relinquishing the leader's jersey had been a strategic move by the team. The U.S. Postal team's plan was to stay near the front of the pack in the early stages and to conserve energy for the crucial time trial stages and the Alps. Said Osipow, "There've been years when we would have killed to defend that jersey. But not now. It's not worth our energy. We'll need that in the Alps."[55]

## The Race of Truth

The time trial in Metz was known as the Race of Truth because it eliminates pretenders to the overall title. At 56 kilometers (35 miles), it was much longer than the brief Prologue and gave the stronger riders a chance to make up—or lose—significant chunks of time. The racers started out in staggered fashion, at two-minute intervals. The early leader was Zülle of Switzerland, who finished in just over 1:09:00.

When it was Armstrong's turn, he started out at a terrific pace. It was not long before he passed prerace favorite Olano, who had crashed and lost about thirty seconds. Armstrong passed other riders who had also crashed. Pedaling ever faster, he passed Tom Steels of Belgium, who had started out six minutes before him. Through the radio he carried with him, Armstrong heard Bruyneel screaming, "You're blowing up the Tour de France!"[56]

Armstrong's pace eventually took its toll, and he labored toward the finish. Still, he crossed the line in a time of 1:08:36, nearly a full minute ahead of Zülle. Armstrong once more wore the yellow jersey.

## The Mountains

Armstrong headed into the mountain stages with a lead of 2:20. This could evaporate very quickly, however. Teamwork and strategy in these Alpine stages were crucial. In order to conserve energy for the later big climbs, Armstrong needed to draft behind his teammates.

Stage 9—the first mountain stage—finished in the town of Sestrière, Italy, with three large peaks along the way. After the third peak, Armstrong was part of a group of five riders who trailed the two leaders—Ivan Gotti and Fernando Escartin—by about twenty-five seconds. With 8 kilometers (5 miles) to go to Sestrière, Armstrong made his move. He accelerated through a curve and began gaining on the leaders. He moved past Gotti and then caught Escartin. He surged past, leaving a widening gap with the former leaders far behind. As Bruyneel kept him informed of his progress on their two-way radios, Armstrong continued pushing to increase his lead. He finished first, far ahead of the pack heading into Sestrière, and now led the Tour by 6:03. "I think before today there were some questions about my abilities in the mountains," said Armstrong, "so I think it was important to show that the team and I are strong in the mountains."[57]

*Armstrong stamped his authority on the 1999 Tour de France with dominant rides in the Alps and Pyrenees. Here, he leads second-place-overall Alex Zülle up a climb.*

## Drugs

Armstrong and his teammates continued to hold the lead through the transition stages of the Tour extending from the Alps to the Pyrenees. His success in the Alps, however, aroused suspicions in the French press. Many could not believe he could be so strong after his ordeal with cancer. They hinted that he must be on drugs and even speculated that his chemotherapy treatments had somehow helped him.

Drug use had become an increasingly contentious topic of the Tour. Just the year before, in 1998, controversy over drug use had disrupted the Tour in an unprecedented way. That year, French police found supplies of EPO (a hormone that stimulates the production of oxygen-rich red blood cells) and anabolic steroids hidden in several team cars. Many riders and team officials were arrested and sent to jail for using the performance-enhancing drugs. With a cloud of suspicion hanging over everyone, one team was expelled from the race, and six other teams quit in protest. Armstrong sympathized with the riders who had been caught, but he believed the scandal would ensure a fairer race from that point on.

For years rumors had circulated through biking circles that some racers were using drugs to improve their performances. As Armstrong wrote, "Doping is an unfortunate fact of life in cycling, or any other endurance sport for that matter. Inevitably, some teams and riders feel . . . that they have to do it to stay competitive within the peloton."[58]

For the 1999 Tour, Armstrong had passed every required drug test. Still the rumors that his spectacular performance was due to drug use refused to die. Following Stage 15—the first stage through the Pyrenees—the newspaper *Le Monde* published a story stating that Armstrong had tested positive for a banned substance. That substance was in a cortisone cream he needed for a case of saddle sores. The cream had been cleared with Tour authorities before the race had started, and Tour officials issued a statement affirming Armstrong's innocence.

Nonetheless the accusations began to have a demoralizing effect on Armstrong. He was hurt that the French journalists, in particular, were so suspicious. As he told them, "I live in France, I race the whole year in France, my Tour de France preparation was done in France. If I want to dope, that would be ridiculous."[59]

Armstrong was determined not to let the accusations take his mind off his goal. He continued to protect his lead through the final stages of the Tour. Following the last mountain stage, the International Cycling Union (ICU) released the results of all his drug tests. With no evidence whatsoever hinting at illegal drug use, Tour organizer Jean-Marie Leblanc gave Armstrong a vote of confidence. Said Leblanc, "Armstrong beating his illness is a sign that the Tour can beat its own illness. It was incredibly symbolic. Armstrong's personal story is all to do with cycling values like tenacity and courage."[60]

## A Final Challenge

After three weeks and 2,200 miles (3,542km), Armstrong led the Tour by 6:15. One last obstacle stood in the way of a victory: the Stage 19 final time trial in the town of Futuroscope. Stage 19 was a 57-kilometer-long race. Rather than play it safe and protect his lead instead of taking chances, Armstrong decided to go all out. He wanted to become the fourth rider to ever sweep all the time trials in the Tour.

When it was Armstrong's turn, he began as if he had been shot from a cannon. He passed the first three time checks with the best mark, but he began to tire over the last six kilometers (3.75 miles). Determined not to be denied, he pushed his body to its limit. He raced down the final straightaway and crossed the finish line with a time of 1:08:17. He had won by 9 seconds. Victory in the Tour was assured, with his closest competitor more than 7:30 behind him in the overall standings.

## Paris

According to tradition, the final stage of the Tour de France is a 99-mile (159-km), largely ceremonial ride from Arpajon to the capital of Paris. The peloton travels at an unhurried pace until reaching the Arc de Triomphe. At that point the victorious team rides to the front and then sprints ten laps over a course in the city's center. The race ends with a postrace victory lap.

*A triumphant Armstrong poses with his wife (left) and mother on the Champs Elysées after winning the 1999 Tour.*

As Armstrong and U.S. Postal teammates rode into Paris, the Champs Elysées was closed to traffic and filled with hundreds of thousands of spectators lining the avenue and cheering for the riders. The riders picked up speed for the final ten-lap sprint to the finish. When Armstrong crossed the finish line, his dream officially became a reality: He had won the Tour de France.

Armstrong was ushered to the podium where the victory ceremony was held. After receiving the trophy, he ran into the stands to embrace his wife and his mother. He then rejoined his teammates for the ceremonial victory lap along the Champs Elysées. Later, while speaking to the members of the media who had gathered, he summarized his feelings. "I would just like to say one thing," he said. "If you ever get a second chance in life for something, you've got to go all the way."[61]

# Chapter 6

# Continued Success

W HEN ARMSTRONG RETURNED to Austin following his victory in the Tour, he was greeted as a conquering hero. He had accomplished an amazing feat against overwhelming odds. He was invited to the Texas state capitol to meet Governor—and future president—George W. Bush. Armstrong was besieged with offers

*In 1999 Armstrong presents a yellow jersey to then-governor of Texas George W. Bush. Austin held a parade to honor Armstrong's Tour victory.*

from countless companies eager to cash in on the revenue generated by his victory. Less than three months after Armstrong's victory, he celebrated again, when his first child, Luke David, was born.

Armstrong thrived on new challenges. Having won the Tour de France, his new goal was to win it a second time. As coaches are fond of telling players on a championship team, as hard as it is to win a title, it is even harder to repeat. The incentive to win is not quite the same, and players often become complacent. In Armstrong's case, his family and his newfound celebrity were taking up more and more of his time. Few people thought he would be able to overcome these obstacles to return to the winner's podium. Their doubts were all the incentive Armstrong needed. "Watch," he told his friends. "I'm going to win it again. And you know why? Because none of them think I can."[62]

In May of 2000, Armstrong accompanied the other members of the U.S. Postal team on a series of training camps in the Alps and Pyrenees. They began familiarizing themselves with the routes they would be following in the Tour. Despite being hospitalized on one of these practice runs when his front tire hit a rock and threw him off the bike, Armstrong faced the 2000 Tour confident of his chances for success.

Armstrong went on to win four more races over the following four years. These races provided some of the most memorable moments in Tour history and offered vivid examples of Armstrong's increasing maturity, as an athlete, as a biking strategist, and as a man.

## A Second Tour Victory and a Third Olympic Disappointment

The 2000 Tour de France was the eighty-seventh in the event's long history. For Armstrong it proceeded much as the 1999 Tour had. He finished second in the Prologue, losing the top spot to David Millar by just two seconds. The opening, flat stages of the race were held in almost continuous rain. Rather than pushing for the lead, Armstrong was content to remain in contention, saving his energy for the grueling mountain stages. There he was sure his preparation would give him an advantage.

## A Change in Technique

Armstrong changed his pedaling technique when he returned to cycling after his bout with cancer. His coach Chris Carmichael, explained in a 2003 interview:

> Since his comeback from cancer, we have done a lot of work on his pedaling technique. Where he used to grind up hills in a big gear, he now spins up them by pedaling faster in smaller gears. It still takes the same amount of work to get up the mountain, but now he is breaking that work into smaller pieces, meaning each pedal stroke is less strenuous than before. . . .
>
> By pedaling faster instead of harder, Armstrong can ascend comfortably with other elite climbers while their legs are burning with lactic acid. . . . He can attack hard and leave them behind because he trained his aerobic system to bear the brunt of the climbing work instead of his legs. When it is time to accelerate toward the finish line, his legs will still have the power to propel him to a fifth Tour de France victory.

By the end of the first mountain stage, Armstrong had taken over first place. The race was not over, however, and, as the cyclists knew, anything could happen in the unpredictable mountains. Armstrong found that out during the last mountain stage when he made a mistake that jeopardized his pursuit of a second Tour victory. While trying to keep up with former Tour winner Marco Pantani of Italy, Armstrong passed through one of the feed zones without getting something to eat. With about six miles to go, his strength gave out. He began to dehydrate and almost became delirious. Somehow he was able to keep going.

Amazingly, Armstrong crossed the finish line having lost just ninety seconds off his lead. He maintained his lead through the final flat stages as the riders made their way toward Paris. He recuperated enough to win the last time trial with the second-fastest time in the Tour's history. Armstrong rode into Paris, where he climbed the winner's podium for the second time. "Armstrong is a worthy champion" said runner-up Jan Ullrich of Germany. "He was the strongest man, and he met out every attack. He earned his victory."[63] Added Frenchman Laurent Jalabert, "Lance so dominated the race that he has absolutely become the boss of the Tour. He may not have won lots of stages, but at every crucial moment he was clearly above the others."[64]

Armstrong had little time to savor his second Tour victory. The following month he suffered a serious injury while biking near Nice, France. He rode head-on into a car coming around a blind curve and suffered a fractured vertebra. Doctors advised him against riding for a while, but Armstrong insisted he was going to race in the Sydney Olympics that September. He rested for a couple weeks, then returned to his training regimen, determined to make up for the disappointments he had suffered in the 1992 and 1996 Olympiads. However, the gold medal eluded him again in 2000.

In the 148-mile (238-km) road race, he finished in thirteenth place; in the 29-mile (47-km) event, he came in third to win the bronze medal. Armstrong refused to make excuses for his showing. "I felt good," he told the gathered media. "I can't say that I had any major problems. No mechanical problems, no discomfort on the course, no problem with the neck. My preparation was good. I have no excuses. I gave everything and I got third place. The two riders in front of me were better and faster and stronger." [65]

## A Third Tour Victory

The 2001 Tour de France proved to be more difficult than the previous two. Several members of the U.S. Postal team suffered injuries, limiting their ability to help Armstrong. He found himself well back in the standings as the riders entered the mountain stages of the race. Bruyneel wanted Armstrong to fake fatigue in order to fool the other teams. In this way Bruyneel hoped the leading team would race harder in an effort to put him away, while unwittingly expending more energy on the early climbs.

The plan worked to perfection. "All the team managers have a TV in their car," said Armstrong, "so they must have thought I was in trouble on the [Col du] Glandon. Well, they were wrong." [66] As he reached the bottom of the famed L'Alpe d'Huez—the final peak of Stage 10—Armstrong began to accelerate. He shot past one rider after another until finally overtaking the exhausted leader of the stage, Laurent Roux.

Armstrong rode the final stage into Paris assured of his third consecutive Tour win. Afterward he expressed his goals for the future. "I've felt better this year than any year," he said. "It's almost as if things are on cruise control. Even though there may appear to be a lot of disruptions in this sport, in this team, in my family and my life, to me things are very even. I love the job I do. I love to be competitive and race a bike—literally race the bike every day. That's what keeps me coming back. I'll be back next year. And it won't be to finish second." [67]

## A Fourth Tour Victory

Armstrong's training regimen for the 2002 Tour was a year-round program, with no off-season. The brutal training schedule gave him a valuable edge over the other riders. As he wrote, "To my way of thinking, the Tour wasn't won in July, it was won by riding when other people weren't willing to." [68]

The 2002 Tour de France was somewhat shorter, but more severe, than the 2001 race, with four important mountain stages among the final eight. Many were convinced this was done to prevent Armstrong from running away with the competition. The U.S. Postal team, however, proved to be stronger than ever. Armstrong took over the Tour lead in Stage 11, and Big Blue, as the team was known, kept the pressure on the other squads. Explained Spanish rider Joseba Beloki, who had finished third overall in each of the past two years, "Basically, it's like following a jackhammer. . . . It was clear there was no way I was going to follow that speed." [69]

By the end of Stage 14, the race, for all intents and purposes, had already been decided. Armstrong rode into Paris with his fourth *consecutive* Tour victory, a feat accomplished by only three other riders: Anquetil, Merckx, and Induráin. The U.S. Postal team had run a nearly perfect race, with not a single tactical error. Armstrong finished with a winning margin of 7:17, completing the course in just over eighty-two hours.

## A Fifth Tour Victory, Tying the Greats

The 2003 Tour marked the event's one hundredth anniversary. Armstrong won the race while overcoming a series of physical woes that included tendinitis (inflammation in a tendon or the tendon's covering) in his legs, a stomach virus, and severe dehydration, and mishaps including a 176-bike pileup in Stage 1, a faulty brake in Stage 10, and an accident caused by a child on the course. The manner in which Armstrong avoided another accident dur-

*Acknowledging the cheers of fans as he rides on the Champs Elysées in 2002, Armstrong celebrates his fourth consecutive Tour victory.*

ing Stage 9 has become a part of Tour de France lore. Eric Hagerman describes the incident:

> Rival Joseba Beloki went down hard in front of Armstrong on the descent into Gap. That tricky little maneuver you've seen a hundred times by now—when Armstrong shot off a switchback to avoid Beloki sprawled on the molten asphalt, aimed his bike down a hassocky hillside, executed a cyclocross dismount to clear the ditch separating him from the road, then slipped right back into the group of contenders—will stand as one of those signal moments in sports that utterly defines an athlete's character. [70]

## The Racer's Edge

In a sport where seconds can determine the difference between winning and losing, the bikes that are used are as important a factor as the racers themselves. Over the years Armstrong has had five bike sponsors: Merlin, Eddy Merckx, Caloi, Fondriest, and Trek. He currently uses bikes manufactured by Trek Bicycles, a company founded in Waterloo, Wisconsin, in 1976.

Different bikes are manufactured for time trials, mountain racing, and road racing. Armstrong has his own team of designers, engineers, and aerospace experts working to produce the ultimate riding machine. According to *Bicycling* magazine, his development team spent more than $1 million to help him gain a few seconds of mechanical advantage in the 2004 Tour de France. A few grams less weight, or slightly less aerodynamic drag, is sometimes enough to separate the champions from the also-rans at racing's highest level. As Armstrong explained in a release issued by the Wisconsin Technology Network, "Competing in a race such as the Tour de France demands using every resource to remain ahead of the competition, and AMD's [a manufacturer of computer processors] superior technology has enabled Trek to design standard road, climbing and time trial bicycles that are truly cutting-edge."

*With every second critical, a mechanic makes a speedy adjustment to Armstrong's Trek bicycle after a crash in the 2004 Tour.*

When Ullrich crashed during the final time trial stage, Armstrong's victory was assured. His sixty-one-second margin of victory was the narrowest of any of his five wins. Armstrong joined Anquetil, Merckx, Hinault, and Induráin as the Tour's only five-time winners. Only Armstrong and Induráin, however, won all five in a row.

Armstrong attributed some of his success to the many cancer patients he had met and spoken to. "I take inspiration from these people," he said. "It's almost an unfair advantage that I get to talk to these people every day."[71]

## Continuing Drug Rumors

Throughout Armstrong's dazzling career, people continued to find it hard to believe that he could achieve such feats without using illegal drugs of some kind. Armstrong welcomed the frequent drug tests because they offered the only possible proof of his innocence. Despite passing every single test, however, Armstrong still had detractors who insisted he must be using some illegal substance.

Shortly after returning from the 2000 Olympics, for example, Armstrong was rocked by the announcement that he was under criminal investigation for doping by the French authorities. During the Tour someone had videotaped a member of his medical staff disposing of trash bags. The authorities hinted the bags may have contained "medical waste" that would have incriminated him. The U.S. Postal team spokesman issued an angry denial, but Armstrong continued to come under close scrutiny from the French press.

Armstrong believed the investigation had begun, in part, because of a strong anti-American sentiment. Many resented the idea of an American winning the Tour. Armstrong was deeply hurt by the accusations. He loved France and had lived there for part of each year since 1997. He tried to speak the language and made every effort to fit in with the natives, but apparently it was not enough to quell the rumors.

The U.S. Postal team gave French judicial investigators urine samples. The ICU announced it would conduct its own tests. Armstrong looked forward to being cleared of the charges, because he said he knew he had not used any illegal substances. Incredibly, even though no evidence of doping came up, it was not good enough for the investigator in charge of the French investigation. "The scientific expert who does the tests thinks he has overlooked something," the French police investigator told team director Bruyneel. "He says it's not possible that there is nothing." [72] Incensed, Armstrong decided to leave France and move to Spain.

The investigation continued through the winter. The prosecutors insisted additional tests were needed but refused to clear Armstrong when the new results showed no indication of drug use. With the cloud of suspicion still hanging over his head, Armstrong prepared for the 2001 Tour. The investigation dragged on for more than two years. It found no evidence of doping by Armstrong.

# Chapter 7

# Seeking a Record-Setting Victory

ARMSTRONG'S QUEST FOR an unprecedented sixth Tour de France victory began amid controversy. The five-time champion entered the race as the odds-on favorite, but the rumors that his victories were fueled by illegal substances continued to flourish. In 2004 a new book—*L.A. Confidential: The Secrets of Lance Armstrong*—accused Armstrong of using performance-enhancing drugs before and during the 1999 Tour. The book's publication thrust the lingering rumors about Armstrong back into the spotlight. Two French newspapers published excerpts from the book about a month prior to the start of the race. Irish sportswriter David Walsh, one of the book's authors, admitted the case against Armstrong was based on circumstantial evidence. "We don't actually prove anything," he said. "We just set out the facts and let the reader decide for himself who's telling the truth. But we do give names for every accusation." [73]

Many of the accusations were attributed to Emma O'Reilly, who was a physiotherapist (a therapist who treats injuries and disabilities with exercises) with the U.S. Postal team for several years before being fired for what was termed "inappropriate behavior." Among other things, she said Armstrong asked her for makeup to cover bruises on his arm caused by injections of illegal substances. She said Armstrong gave her a bag of empty syringes to dispose of following a 1998 race. She also said she delivered a bag of pills to him during a 1999 training camp in the Pyrenees.

"[Armstrong] said he had used a steroid before or during the Route du Sud the month before [the 1999 Tour] and he thought

*Physiotherapist Emma O'Reilly, seen here massaging one of Armstrong's teammates, accused Armstrong of using performance-enhancing drugs during the 1999 Tour.*

it would be O.K. for the Tour," O'Reilly contended in the book. "He thought the drug would be completely eliminated from his body." When the drug was detected during tests, O'Reilly contended, the cream Armstrong had used for saddle sores was said to be the source. Armstrong later reportedly told her, "Now, Emma, you know enough to destroy me." [74]

Armstrong vehemently denied the allegations. He filed libel suits against the book's authors and the newspapers that published the excerpts. "This isn't the first time I've lived through this," he said. "I heard it in 1999, 2001, 2003—it happens all of the time, and every time we've chose to sit back and let it pass. But we've reached a point where we can't tolerate it any more. We're going to do everything we can to fight them." [75]

The controversy might have been viewed as a distraction for a man trying to win his sixth Tour crown. But Patrick Lefevere, the highly respected manager of the Quick Step cycling team, suggested otherwise. The controversy ignited by the book's allegations might provide Armstrong additional motivation, he said.

"I think that Lance is very angry, and it will be his rivals at the Tour who feel the full brunt of that anger."[76] Clearly, Lefevere understood Lance Armstrong.

## A New Tour Course

The course for the 2004 Tour de France was unusual. Two individual time trials were scheduled for the last week, rather than being spread out over the three-week period as is typical. One of the time trials was the climb at L'Alpe d'Huez, famed for its difficulty. By setting up the Tour in this way, the Tour directors hoped to keep the race close until the very end.

Many people expressed doubts about Armstrong's chances of winning this kind of Tour. They questioned whether someone his age—thirty-two—would be able to perform well in two time trials in the grueling mountain stages. Nevertheless, Armstrong

### The Dark Side of Cycling

The 1998 Tour de France is remembered for the doping scandal that resulted in the arrests of several participants. It was not the first time, however, that rumors of drugs had touched the sport of cycling. The history of modern doping, in fact, begins with the six-day bicycling craze of the 1890s. In this indoor event, riders raced continuously with only brief stops for rest and refreshments. The winner was the racer who covered the greatest distance in the 144 hours.

The six-day bicyclists of that period experimented with ways of alleviating exhaustion. As reported by Tom Donohoe and Neil Johnson in their book, *Foul Play: Drug Abuse in Sports,* "The riders' black coffee was 'boosted' with extra caffeine and peppermint, and as the race progressed the mixture was spiked with increasing doses of cocaine and strychnine [both stimulants]. Brandy was also frequently added to cups of tea. Following the sprint sequences of the race, nitroglycerine capsules were often given to the cyclists to ease breathing difficulties." (Nitroglycerine dilates the arteries to increase blood flow.)

When the Tour de France came along in 1903, the experimentation continued. Wrote German sports journalist Hans Halter, "For as long as the Tour has existed, since 1903, its participants have been doping themselves. No dope, no hope. The Tour, in fact, is only possible because—not despite the fact—there is doping. For 60 years this was allowed. For the past 30 years it has been officially prohibited. Yet the fact remains: great cyclists have been doping themselves, then as now."

was still the favorite to win going into the race. German Ullrich, Spaniards Roberto Heras and Iban Mayo, and Americans Tyler Hamilton and Levi Leipheimer were expected to be his main competition.

Armstrong began his "Quest for Six" by recording the second-best time in the Prologue, trailing only Fabian Cancellara of Switzerland. Said Armstrong, "It's just a start. . . . There is a lot of dangerous racing to go. Just in three days, we have some sections of cobblestones, that if it rains and is windy, will be very dangerous." [77] His words proved to be prophetic.

The next three stages—from Liège to Charleroi, Charleroi to Namur, and Waterloo to Wasquehal—were marked by rain and wind and numerous crashes. As Armstrong later recounted, "I don't remember a Tour with so many crashes in the first week. It seemed like every time you turned around you'd hear over the radio 'Oh!—Crash in the peloton.'" [78] Mayo was among those injured in the mishaps, leading him to proclaim, "The Tour is lost for me." [79]

The Stage 4 team time trial—a forty-mile course from Cambrai to Arras—was a resounding success for the U.S. Postal squad. Despite riding in a heavy rain, the team recorded the third-fastest team time trial in Tour history. Armstrong and four of his teammates occupied the top five spots on the leader board for the stage. The team's strategy was to simply remain in contention through the next several stages, preserving energy for the mountains. As a result the race would be decided that final week.

More bad weather and poor road conditions continued to take their toll on the riders. Hamilton, one of Armstrong's main rivals, was injured in a crash coming into Angers. Eight different teams had lost at least one rider each due to crashes and injuries through seven stages. As Bruyneel said, "We get on narrow roads, it's windy sometimes, rainy, so really the first goal is stay out of trouble, and not have any crashes and that's not easy to do." [80]

## Mountains and Controversy

As the race moved into the Pyrenees, Thomas Voeckler of France held the lead in the overall standings. Armstrong was in sixth place, approximately 9:30 off the pace. He began to make his

*A Norwegian cyclist winces in pain after a bad crash in the 2004 Tour. The opening stages of that year's Tour were marred by a large number of crashes.*

move in Stage 12, which began in the town of Castelsarrasin and finished with an ascent to the La Mongie ski station in the French Pyrenees. Armstrong finished second, making up almost half the deficit. He cut further into Voeckler's lead by winning Stage 13, a 127.7-mile (205.5-km) trek consisting of seven climbs through the mountains from Lannemezan to Plateau du Beille.

With U.S. Postal riding extremely well, Armstrong took over the yellow jersey with a victory in Stage 15, the first one in the Alps. At the end of the seven-climb, 112-mile (180-km) journey through the mountains, he had enough left to outlast rivals Ivan Basso and Ullrich in a sprint to the finish. From that point on, there was no stopping Armstrong in the Tour's final week.

Prior to the individual time trial at L'Alpe d'Huez in Stage 16, Armstrong had received threats against his life. Security was stepped up, and Armstrong was flanked by agents during the climb. Despite the precautions, several unruly spectators booed, yelled at, and spat at Armstrong and some of the other riders. Race director Leblanc later admitted, "I can understand why Armstrong

said the [16th] stage had made him feel uneasy. Now we know why. He had good reason to fear for his security. He had received threats, whether they were founded or not I don't know."[81]

Armstrong still managed to win the time trial at L'Alpe d'Huez and further increase his lead in the overall standings. He covered the 9.6 miles (15.5km) of hairpin bends in 39:41, for an average speed of 14.5 miles (23.3km) per hour. He could not understand, however, the reason for the negative reactions of the fans:

> People boo, but what do they want? Do they want a champion who doesn't work hard? It doesn't make sense for them to boo me but to cheer a rider [Frenchman Richard Virenque] who was involved in the biggest doping case in cycling. But then we're racing in a country where they like the rider who comes second more than the rider who finishes first.[82]

Another incident occurred during Stage 18, on the run from Annemasse to Lons-le-Saunier. Italian rider Filippo Simeoni had been at odds with Armstrong over claims regarding doping among the riders and the role played by sports doctor Michele Ferrari, with whom Armstrong had ties. Simeoni had admitted to taking dope as an amateur while under Ferrari's guidance. When Simeoni began to speed ahead of the pack, Armstrong chased after him, even though he was no threat to Armstrong's status as leader. The other riders in the pack let Simeoni know he was not welcome, because Armstrong's presence in front meant their chances of winning the stage were minimal. A bitter Simeoni later accused Armstrong of threatening him.

## Glory Once More

Armstrong's victory in Stage 19 assured him of the overall championship. He won the time trial over the rolling 34.1-mile (54.8-km) course in Besançon by more than a minute over second-place finisher Ullrich. The stage win was Armstrong's fifth, for a new personal record.

A rapt throng cheered as the U.S. Postal team made its victory run down the Champs Elysées in the final stage. Flags of the United States and Texas waved among the crowd. Fans came out in droves to witness the historic moment. With that, Armstrong rewrote the history books, becoming the first six-time winner of the Tour de France in the event's long history.

As Armstrong stood on the top step of the Tour podium following his victory, he reflected on the stresses involved with his record-breaking race:

> I was thinking that I was glad to get it over with. There were a lot of pressures before the race and a lot of pressure during the race and a lot of threats, shall we call them, during the race and I was just really glad to make it through number one, alive; number two, as the winner. And then I was just ready to take the crown and take the history book with me. Then I just wanted to get out of there. I don't mean that in a bad way, but it was just . . . the victory was secure and I was ready to leave.[83]

Armstrong won by a margin of 6:19. Andreas Klöden of Germany came in second, followed by Basso and Ullrich. The margin of victory underscored Armstrong's dominance. In 2003 he had won by sixty-one seconds. He admitted that he had not been in the best of shape the previous year. "I paid the price," said Armstrong, "and learned a valuable lesson, and I won't ever make that mistake again." [84]

*Armstrong raises six fingers to represent his six consecutive Tour wins at the start of the final stage of the 2004 Tour.*

When questioned about the 2004 race, Armstrong explained,

I think the biggest difference is in my head, the morale and the motivation, the pure joy of racing. It's as if I was with my five friends and we were 13 years old and we all had new bikes and we said: "Okay, we're going to race from here to there." You want to beat your friends more than anything. You're sprinting and you're attacking. It was like that for me this year, a simple pleasure.[85]

In an interview, Armstrong expressed his further thoughts on the Tour:

It was . . . surprisingly easier than I thought it was going to be. I had prepared myself for what I had thought was going to be a fight for seconds on the clock and it ended up being like 2001 or 2002 where it was a question of minutes. And I think we didn't expect that. I came into the Tour very motivated, incredibly motivated. And with all the heart and intensity that I could and I was surprised that the other guys were so far off. Riders we had expected . . . either Ullrich or Mayo or Hamilton . . . a lot of guys. But then you had other guys come up and make it exciting, like Basso and Klöden. But I was surprised that those people were not such a factor.[86]

------------------------------------------------

# Chapter 8

# A Legacy on and Beyond the Bike

ARMSTRONG UNDERSTOOD THE combined power his cycling career and his victory over cancer presented. He immediately saw that the two accomplishments made him a spokesman for cancer patients everywhere. "In the USA," said Armstrong, "winning the Tour gave me a platform to do what I wanted to do."[87] The fact that he was able to not only compete in, but win, the Tour de France meant that others, too, could beat the disease and live fulfilling lives. It was a message he felt driven to deliver to every member of the cancer community.

Armstrong traveled to hospitals around the country, talking to others who suffered from the illness. His experiences helped him formulate a clearer plan for the goals of his foundation:

> All of these issues fell under the title "survivorship," a curious, post-traumatic state of being that I was experiencing, and which all cancer survivors experience in one form or another. Survivorship, I decided, should be the core of the cancer foundation I'd launched: managing the illness and its aftereffects was as important as fighting it. The Lance Armstrong Foundation began to take shape as a place where people could come for information of the most personal and practical kind. There were other, richer foundations and more comprehensive Web sites, but at the LAF, hopefully you could call or e-mail us and get a greeting card from me to a patient, or you could ask, what's the right exercise for breast-cancer patients and survivors?[88]

In October 2001 Armstrong achieved a victory that must have meant more than any of his Tour de France wins. That fall Armstrong marked his five-year cancer anniversary. That is, he had been free of the disease for five years—an important milestone for cancer patients. When tests showed no recurrence of the disease, Nichols told him, "Your chances of ever having trouble

## The Tour of Hope

In 2003 Bristol-Myers Squibb, in partnership with Lance Armstrong, sponsored the first annual Tour of Hope. The Tour is a weeklong biking journey across the United States undertaken by a team of twenty people who have been touched in some way by cancer. Riders include cancer survivors and their family members, medical professionals, and researchers.

The twenty team members are divided into four squads of five riders each. Team members ride in relays of four- to five-hour segments each day. The time varies with conditions such as weather, terrain, and rider fatigue. Along the way, riders share their stories at local cancer center events in an effort to teach the communities about the benefits of cancer research. Although riders are not required to raise funds, many use the Tour as an opportunity to do so.

*Lance Armstrong (right) leads the 2003 Tour of Hope, a cross-country ride to raise public awareness of cancer research.*

with this again are in essence zero. You need to put this disease out of your mind, in terms of your own cancer."[89]

At home in Austin, Armstrong and his friends and family celebrated with a party. In the back of his mind, however, doubts remained:

> The battle with cancer is started and ended, and won and lost, on a cellular level, and I was worried that the disease could lie dormant, hide out, and come back in ten years, or 20 years, just when I had strolled off into the sunset. I didn't ever want to disrespect the illness, or its track record. You could never turn your back on it.[90]

Armstrong's ever-present thoughts about the disease filled him with a constant sense of being pressed for time, of having to do everything right away because he might not have the chance to do so later. He felt the pressure in his career and in his family life. In November 2001, his family expanded when Kik gave birth to twin girls, Grace Elizabeth and Isabelle Rose.

*Kristen and Lance Armstrong hold their three children on the Champs Elysées after his 2002 Tour de France victory.*

## The Lance Armstrong Foundation Manifesto

The Lance Armstrong Foundation published a manifesto to describe its mission. A portion of it reads:

"We believe in life.

Your life.

And that you must not let cancer take control of it.

We believe in your right to live without pain and, if it comes to it, your right to die with dignity.

We believe in energy: channeled and fierce.

We believe in focus: getting smart and living strong.

Because we're passionate about helping you live every minute of your life with every ounce of your being. . . .

We're about the hard stuff.

Like knowing the first doctor you talk to is not God.

Like finding the nerve and getting the number to get a second opinion.

And a third or even a fourth, if that's what it takes.

We're also about the practical issues of life after treatment.

Cancer may leave your body, but it never leaves your life.

We're your champion on Capitol Hill. Your advocate in the back halls of the healthcare system and your sponsor in the research labs.

When you're cancer-free, the fight has only just begun.

This is the Lance Armstrong Foundation.

Founded and inspired by one of the toughest survivors on the planet.

Live Strong."

The disease, he found, had changed his feelings about practically everything, including the house he had recently built:

> The home, I put a lot into it both in time and money, and I really feel an attachment to this house because this was dirt before, this was level ground and we built it up, furnished it, did everything exactly the way I wanted it. When I started it, I must have been 22 and it showed that a 22-year-old can work hard, financially do well and take on a big project like this and succeed. I've enjoyed it, I enjoy it still. But if it's gone, it's gone.

Now it means a lot less than it did before. Houses, cars, motorcycles, toys, money, fame—it takes on a whole new meaning when you have something like this [cancer]. You realize, "I never lived for that stuff." No, I enjoyed it, but I think something like this makes you not only look at your life, but makes you simplify your life. The home means more than the other things. Before, I would have been devastated if I had to sell it or move out to a little old home built in the '30s, much smaller, not on the lake, not in this price range. That's fine. I could do it. That's fine, I'm alive. That's what it's all about.[91]

## Survivorship

The message of Armstrong and his foundation is one of hope. It is one message he says he will never stop preaching to cancer patients around the world. As he once wrote,

I will always carry the lesson of cancer with me, and feel that I'm a member of the cancer community. I believe I have an obligation to make something better out of my life than before, and to help my fellow human beings who are dealing with the disease. It's a community of shared experience. Anyone who has heard the words "You have cancer" and thought, "Oh, my God, I'm going to die," is a member of it. If you've ever belonged, you never leave.[92]

The mission of the Lance Armstrong Foundation is to provide the practical information and tools people living with cancer need to continue to live strong, productive lives. It serves that mission in four program areas: education, advocacy, public health, and research. Since the foundation was founded in 1997, it has raised more than $34 million toward that mission.

Through the Live Strong program, the foundation educates cancer patients, health-care professionals, and the general public about issues that face cancer patients. It provides information and resources on physical, emotional, and practical topics dealing with all forms of cancer. In addition, survivorship tools help survivors deal with their postcancer lives.

The foundation receives powerful testimonials about its work from cancer survivors. Said one such person, eighteen-year-old Bob Blomquist,

> As a survivor, it can be difficult to understand the impact of cancer on your life. I think it's very important for those of us who live with cancer to share our experience—good or bad—with other survivors and family members. Hearing firsthand about the issues people experience during their ordeal is so compelling and honest, because it's not just about surviving—it's about LIVING and living strong.[93]

The foundation also sponsors initiatives to help the cancer community be heard in Washington, D.C. It increases awareness about health policy issues facing those living with cancer and

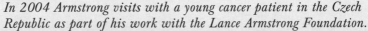
*In 2004 Armstrong visits with a young cancer patient in the Czech Republic as part of his work with the Lance Armstrong Foundation.*

## LiveStrong

In February 2004, officials at Nike began a campaign to commemorate Armstrong's bid for a record sixth Tour de France win and to support his foundation's work improving the lives of cancer survivors and their families. With these goals in mind, Nike began marketing yellow rubber wristbands bearing Armstrong's mantra, "LiveStrong."

Since then, more than 21 million bracelets have been sold at a dollar apiece, with all the revenue raised going to the Lance Armstrong Foundation. The yellow wristbands (the color signifies the jersey awarded to the leader of the Tour de France) have been seen adorning the wrists of many public figures, including presidential candidate John Kerry, comedian Robin Williams, and actor Bruce Willis. As Armstrong says on the Nike Web site, "Yellow wakes me up in the morning. Yellow gets me on the bike every day. Yellow has taught me the true meaning of sacrifice. Yellow makes me suffer. Yellow is the reason I'm here."

*Armstrong's girlfriend Sheryl Crow and cycling fan Robin Williams sport the yellow "LiveStrong" wristbands at the 2004 Tour.*

their families. In May 2002, Armstrong was appointed by President Bush as a member of the Presidential Cancer Panel. The panel monitors the activities of the National Cancer Program, which was a product of the 1971 National Cancer Act signed into law by President Richard M. Nixon. The goal of the legislation was to greatly accelerate the pace of cancer research and its translation into treatments.

In the field of public health, the foundation develops and funds programs that provide after-treatment support for cancer survivors. It works to make people more aware of how to prevent secondary cancers and to promote treatments to ensure healthy lives for survivors. The foundation also funds research on testicular cancer and ways to improve the quality of life for cancer survivors.

Armstrong has enjoyed the riches and fame of his cycling career and foundation work, but he has also been forced to confront the strains of celebrity and the grueling training schedule that has made him a champion cyclist. The training regimen has meant that Armstrong seldom had time to be with his wife and three young children.

In December 2003, the couple divorced. Soon afterward, he began seeing singer Sheryl Crow, who came to his 2004 Tour de France race. Armstrong's image was wounded by his decision to leave the woman who had seen him through his cancer fight and his three young children. Some fans believed he had sacrificed these people for his career. Armstrong himself discussed the turmoil in his personal life:

> I am bitterly disappointed that my marriage failed. It is not what you sign up to. It is not what you sign up to when you have kids. We got together at a weird time. I was coming back from cancer and getting back into sport. I don't know. Marriages are tough. Relationships are tough. I'm here with Sheryl now and it's great, but there is no such thing as a day when everything is rosy all the time. Life's not like that.
>
> My ex-wife and I are trying to get to that place where we're a divorced couple, we're never going to get back together but we can be friends and I can say, "I am father to your children," and she can say, "I am mother to your children" and we try to make it work. [94]

# The Future

Armstrong's 2004 victory naturally led to speculation about his future plans. Some believe Armstrong is headed for a television career. He already has been a television presence on the Outdoor Life Network (OLN), which broadcasts the Tour de France. In 2004 the Discovery Channel signed on to take over sponsorship of his cycling team from the U.S. Postal Service. The corporation has high hopes for its Discovery Health Channel, seemingly a natural fit for him.

The change in sponsorship of the cycling team led many to wonder if Armstrong would return to try for a seventh consecutive win in the Tour. Carmichael has offered this view: "I think he can go as long as he wants, I've never met anybody with the intensity he has." [95]

For months Armstrong sent mixed signals about his intentions. Some comments suggested he was ready to retire. "My personal situation with my children in Texas and me in Europe is the hardest thing for me," he admitted. "This is what will force me to change my schedule. I won't do that again. My kids are 3 years old and 5 years old and they change every three months. I become desperate in the end because they're so far away." [96]

Other comments suggested he intended to continue professional competition. "I have said that I'd like to ride the Giro d'Italia before I stop," he said. "I'd also like to do the World Championships again and attempt the hour record [held by Britain's Chris Boardman]. But time's running out." [97] He also signaled that he was not ready to abandon the Tour de France. "This is the greatest bike race in the world," he said in late 2004. "It's the one that matters the most and the one I love the most. I cannot imagine skipping the Tour. If I come back, it'll be with the perfect conditions and I will come to win." [98] Armstrong finally ended speculation once and for all in February 2005 when he posted on his Web site that he would, indeed, attempt to win a seventh consecutive Tour de France in 2005. He followed up two months later by announcing that he would retire after the race.

Although Armstrong has more Tour victories than anyone, he may still believe he has something to prove to European fans, who still revere the old cycling greats such as Merckx. Merckx is generally considered the greatest cyclist in history since his amazing

445 professional victories included wins in a variety of races, including sprints, time, and long-distance events. "Will the French ever accept Armstrong as a champion of the caliber as their heroes Anquetil, Hinault and Merckx?" the *Washington Post* asked in an article published following his record-setting sixth Tour victory. "'Ah, for that,' said [Daniel] Mangeas, the veteran commentator [who has announced the race for thirty years], 'he'll have to win a seventh Tour.'"[99]

*In 2005, Armstrong's final season in professional cycling, he rode with the newly formed Discovery Channel team.*

## The Legacy

Armstrong's accomplishments changed the face of racing. He brought a relatively obscure sport to the attention of what may be the most sports-conscious nation in the world. His meticulous attention to every detail of the race also changed the essence of the Tour. By employing the latest technology and taking a scientific approach to his training, he has been able to utilize every one of his physical gifts to the utmost. "He's made it more clinical," said rider Bobby Julich. "He's a surgeon, man, and he goes to work." [100]

His success has not put to rest the endless rumors of drug use. As team director Bruyneel said, "It's terribly unfair. He is already winning, and is extremely fit. Still, people always ask that one question: How can he do this without drugs? I understand why people ask, because our sport has been tainted. But Armstrong has a different trick, and I have watched him do it now for four years: he just works harder than anyone else alive." [101]

In 2001, when Armstrong visited the White House, President Bush praised the cyclist's accomplishments both on and off the bike. Armstrong's experiences, Bush said, serve as "a vivid reminder that the great achievements of life are often won or lost in the mountains, when the climb is the steepest, when the heart is tested. . . . He's done more than survive—he has triumphed." [102]

# Notes

---

## Introduction: A Life Fulfilled

1. Lance Armstrong with Sally Jenkins, *It's Not About the Bike*. New York: G.P. Putnam's Sons, 2000, pp. 70–71.
2. Quoted in Lance Armstrong and Graham Watson, *Lance Armstrong: Images of a Champion*. Emmaus, PA: Rodale, 2004.
3. Quoted in Armstrong with Jenkins, *It's Not About the Bike,* p. 38.

## Chapter 1: Childhood in Plano

4. Quoted in Geoff Drake, "Lone Star," *Bicycling,* May 1993.
5. Armstrong with Jenkins, *It's Not About the Bike,* p. 18.
6. Quoted in "Too Tough to Die," *Observer,* September 7, 2003.
7. Quoted in Drake, "Lone Star."
8. Quoted in Michael Specter, "The Long Ride," *New Yorker,* July 15, 2002.
9. Quoted in Armstrong with Jenkins, *It's Not About the Bike,* p. 27.
10. Armstrong with Jenkins, *It's Not About the Bike,* p. 20.
11. Quoted in Geoff Drake, "Lone Star."
12. Quoted in Samuel Abt, *Lance Armstrong's Comeback from Cancer.* San Francisco: Van der Plas, 2000, p. 30.
13. Quoted in Specter, "The Long Ride."
14. Quoted in Abt, *Lance Armstrong's Comeback from Cancer,* p. 26.
15. Quoted in Todd Balf, "Lance vs. Cancer," *Bicycling,* February 1997.
16. Quoted in Sal Ruibal, "Armstrong's Mother Always Part of His Team," *USA Today,* July 27, 2004.
17. Quoted in Specter, "The Long Ride."
18. Quoted in Armstrong with Jenkins, *It's Not About the Bike,* p. 45.
19. Quoted in Drake, "Lone Star."

20. Quoted in Ian Melvin, "The Armstrong Story—Part I," *Roadcycling,* July 1, 2003. www.roadcycling.com.

## Chapter 2: A Young Star

21. Armstrong with Jenkins, *It's Not About the Bike,* p. 51.
22. Quoted in Melvin, "The Armstrong Story–Part I."
23. Quoted in Abt, *Lance Armstrong's Comeback from Cancer,* p. 24.
24. Specter, "The Long Ride."
25. Armstrong with Jenkins, *It's Not About the Bike,* p. 54.
26. Quoted in Abt, *Lance Armstrong's Comeback from Cancer,* p. 28.
27. Quoted in Samuel Abt, "The Big Show," *Bicycling Presents Lance Armstrong,* Issue 43, p. 32.
28. Quoted in Armstrong with Jenkins, *It's Not About the Bike,* p. 62.
29. Armstrong with Jenkins, *It's Not About the Bike,* p. 64.
30. Quoted in Ruibal, "Armstrong's Mother Always Part of His Team."
31. Abt, *Lance Armstrong's Comeback from Cancer,* p. 50.
32. Armstrong with Jenkins, *It's Not About the Bike,* pp. 70–71.

## Chapter 3: Cancer

33. Quoted in Balf, "Lance vs. Cancer."
34. Quoted in Armstrong with Jenkins, *It's Not About the Bike,* p. 12.
35. Quoted in Abt, *Lance Armstrong's Comeback from Cancer,* p. 82.
36. Armstrong with Jenkins, *It's Not About the Bike,* p. 13.
37. Quoted in Nemil Dalal, "Cancer Panelists Inspire Packed Burnham Crowd," *Stanford Daily,* November 9, 2001.
38. Abt, *Lance Armstrong's Comeback from Cancer,* p. 87.
39. Quoted in Armstrong with Jenkins, *It's Not About the Bike,* p. 93.
40. Quoted in Balf, "Lance vs. Cancer."
41. Armstrong with Jenkins, *It's Not About the Bike,* pp. 116–17.
42. Quoted in Abt, *Lance Armstrong's Comeback from Cancer,* p. 85.

## Chapter 4: The Road Back

43. Armstrong with Jenkins, *It's Not About the Bike,* pp. 133–34.
44. Quoted in Balf, "Lance vs. Cancer."
45. Quoted in Armstrong with Jenkins, *It's Not About the Bike,* p. 180.
46. Quoted in Todd Balf, "He's Back and He's Better," *Bicycling,* January/February 1998.

47. Quoted in Peter Joffre Nye, "2nd Chance: The Cycle of Success," *Executive Update,* February 2002.

48. Quoted in Balf, "He's Back and He's Better."

49. Armstrong with Jenkins, *It's Not About the Bike,* p. 191.

50. Quoted in Armstrong with Jenkins, *It's Not About the Bike,* p. 198.

51. Quoted in Balf, "He's Back and He's Better."

52. Quoted in Abt, *Lance Armstrong's Comeback from Cancer,* p. 103.

## Chapter 5: The 1999 Tour de France

53. Quoted in Abt, *Lance Armstrong's Comeback from Cancer,* p. 103.

54. Quoted in Nye, "2nd Chance."

55. Quoted in Abt, *Lance Armstrong's Comeback from Cancer,* p. 122.

56. Armstrong with Jenkins, *It's Not About the Bike,* p. 237.

57. Quoted in Abt, *Lance Armstrong's Comeback from Cancer,* p. 140.

58. Armstrong with Jenkins, *It's Not About the Bike,* p. 205.

59. Quoted in Abt, *Lance Armstrong's Comeback from Cancer,* p. 147.

60. Quoted in Thomas Sancton, "From Despair to Glory," *Time,* July 19, 1999.

61. Quoted in Nye, "2nd Chance."

## Chapter 6: Continued Success

62. Lance Armstrong with Sally Jenkins, *Every Second Counts.* New York: Broadway, 2003, p. 34.

63. Quoted in Shawn Pogatchnik, "Armstrong: An American in Paris Triumphs Again," *SouthCoast Today,* July 24, 2000.

64. Quoted in James Startt, "The New Boss," *Bicycling,* October 2000.

65. Armstrong with Jenkins, *Every Second Counts,* p. 69.

66. Quoted in James Startt, "Lance's Tour," *Bicycling,* October 2001.

67. Quoted in Startt, "Lance's Tour."

68. Armstrong with Jenkins, *Every Second Counts,* p. 147.

69. Quoted in James Startt, "The Blue Train," *Bicycling,* October 2002.

70. Eric Hagerman, "Armstrong's Career Move," *Bicycling,* October 2003.

71. Quoted in Pogatchnik, "Armstrong."

72. Armstrong with Jenkins, *Every Second Counts,* p. 83.

## Chapter 7: Seeking a Record-Setting Victory

73. Quoted in Samuel Abt, "Cycling: Book Details Suspicions About Lance Armstrong and Drug Use," *International Herald Tribune,* June 14, 2004. www.iht.com/articles/524790.html.

74. Quoted in Abt, "Cycling: Book Details Suspicions About Lance Armstrong and Drug Use."

75. Quoted in Steve Donohue, "Riding Along with Lance," *Multichannel News,* June 21, 2004. http://print.google.com/priint/doc? articleid=5fJSQtlcwA.

76. Quoted in "Armstrong Bid to Rewrite Tour History Overshadowed by Doping Claims," Agence France-Presse, July 2, 2004.

77. Quoted in "Armstrong Second in Opening Event," ESPN, July 3, 2004. sports.espn.go.com.

78. Quoted in The Paceline, Web site of the official fan club of Lance Armstrong and the U.S. Postal Service team. www.thepaceline.com.

79. Quoted in Dan Osipow, "Hold the Mayo . . . McEwen Takes the Lead," *Dan Osipow's Notebook,* July 6, 2004, United States Postal Service Pro Cycling Team. www.uspsprocycling.com.

80. Quoted in Dan Osipow, "Pozzato Stays Strong in Final Sprint to Take Stage," *Dan Osipow's Notebook,* July 10, 2004, United States Postal Service Pro Cycling Team. www.uspsprocycling.com.

81. Quoted in "Armstrong Security Beefed Up After Threats," July 24, 2004, Agence France-Presse. www.keepmedia.com.

82. Quoted in Jeremy Whittle, "Armstrong Rides into History After Tour de Force," *The Times* (London), July 26, 2004.

83. Quoted in "My Way: Six and Counting for Armstrong," *Cycling News,* October 26, 2004. www.cyclingnews.com.

84. Quoted in "Lance's Tour de Force," *Sports Illustrated,* July 25, 2004. www.si.com.

85. Quoted in Rupert Guinness, "Armstrong Makes It Six; Boonen Wins on the Champs-Elysees," *VeloNews,* July 25, 2004.

86. Quoted in "My Way: Six and Counting for Armstrong"

## Chapter 8: A Legacy on and Beyond the Bike

87. Quoted in Jeremy Whittle, "Miracle Man," http://bicykle.szm.sk/lance.html.

88. Lance Armstrong with Sally Jenkins, *Every Second Counts,* pp. 13–14.

89. Armstrong with Jenkins, *Every Second Counts,* p. 132.

90. Armstrong with Jenkins, *Every Second Counts,* p. 135.

91. Quoted in Abt, *Lance Armstrong's Comeback from Cancer,* pp. 85–86.

92. Armstrong with Jenkins, *It's Not About the Bike,* p. 274.

93. Quoted in Lance Armstrong Foundation. www.laf.org/about/LAF Annualweb.v3.pdf.

94. Quoted in Alastair Campbell, "A Legend? I Would Rather Be Remembered As a Dad," *UK Times Online,* February 28, 2004. www.timesonline.co.uk.

95. Quoted in Linda Robertson, "With His Record Sixth Tour de France Title Secure, Lance Armstrong Enjoyed a Leisurely Ride Down the Champs-Elysees During the Event's Final Stage," *Miami Herald,* July 26, 2004.

96. Quoted in Ann Killion, "Historic Sixth: Armstrong Is Tour de France's Most-Celebrated Champion," *San Jose (CA) Mercury News,* July 26, 2004.

97. Quoted in Whittle, "Armstrong Rides into History After Tour de Force."

98. Quoted in "Armstrong Has the Hardest Choice After Easiest Tour," *Sports Illustrated,* July 26, 2004. www.si.com.

99. Quoted in Sarah Kaufman, "Tour de Lance," *Washington Post,* July 26, 2004.

100. Quoted in "Rivals Eagerly Await Post-Armstrong Era," *Sports Illustrated,* July 26, 2004. www.si.com.

101. Quoted in Specter, "The Long Ride."

102. Quoted in Nye, "2nd Chance."

# Important Dates in the Life of Lance Armstrong

**September 18, 1971**
Lance Gunderson is born to Eddie and Linda (Mooneyham) Gunderson in Oak Cliff, Texas.

**1974**
Lance is legally adopted by Terry Armstrong, Linda's second husband.

**1987**
He finishes in thirty-second place in the President's Triathlon as a fifteen-year-old.

**1988**
Named "National Rookie of the Year" by *Triathlete* magazine.

**1990**
Competes for the Junior World Cycling Championships squad in Moscow.

**1991**
Named to the U.S. National Cycling Team. He signs with the pro-am Subaru-Montgomery team. He wins the U.S. Amateur Championship and the Settimana Bergamasca.

**1992**
Wins La Vuelta La Ribiera, the First Union Grand Prix, and the Thrift Drug Classic, but finishes in a disappointing fourteenth place in the Barcelona Summer Olympics. He turns pro following the Olympics and finishes last in first pro race.

**1993**

Wins Trophée Laigueglia and the U.S. Triple Crown of Cycling.

**1994**

Wins Thrift Drug Classic and one stage of the Tour DuPont.

**1995**

Armstrong finishes the Tour de France for the first time (thirty-sixth overall), with one stage win. He is named *VeloNews* 1995 "American Male Cyclist of the Year."

**1996**

Armstrong signs a $2.5-million contract to ride for the Cofidis team in 1997. He finishes sixth in the time trials and fourteenth in the road race in the Atlanta Summer Olympics.

**October 2, 1996**

Armstrong is diagnosed with testicular cancer and undergoes surgery to remove the testicle the next day.

**October 25, 1996**

Doctors remove two lesions on Armstrong's brain.

**1997**

Establishes the Lance Armstrong Foundation to benefit cancer research. He holds first annual Ride for the Roses.

**October 16, 1997**

Signs a contract with U.S. Postal Service team.

**1998**

Marries Kristin ("Kik") Richard in May. In return to racing, he finishes fourth in U.S. Pro Championships; finishes fourth in the twenty-three-day-long Vuelta a España; wins Rhineland Pfalz Tour, Ride for the Roses criterium, Cascade Classic, Tour of Luxembourg.

**1999**

Armstrong wins the Tour de France, including four stage wins, despite accusations of drug use. His son, Luke, is born in October.

**2000**

Armstrong wins second consecutive Tour de France, including one stage win. He finishes thirteenth in 148-mile (238-km) Olympic road race, and third (bronze medal) in the 29-mile (47-km) event in the Sydney Summer Olympics. French authorities announce a criminal investigation into drug charges.

## 2001
Wins third consecutive Tour de France, including four stage wins. His twin daughters, Grace and Isabelle, are born.

## 2002
Armstrong wins his fourth consecutive Tour de France, including four stage wins. He is named *Sports Illustrated*'s "Sportsman of the Year."

## 2003
Wins fifth consecutive Tour de France, including two stage wins. He separates from Kristin, whom he divorces later in the year.

## 2004
Armstrong wins a record sixth consecutive Tour de France, including six stage wins.

# For Further Reading

---

## Books

Lance Armstrong and Graham Watson, *Lance Armstrong: Images of a Champion*. Emmaus, PA: Rodale, 2004. A collection of pictures of the six-time Tour de France winner by the sport's premier photographer.

Lance Armstrong, Chris Carmichael, and Peter Joffre Nye, *The Lance Armstrong Performance Program: Seven Weeks to the Perfect Ride*. Emmaus, PA: Rodale, 2000. The ultimate insider's guide to becoming a better rider, based on the regimen Carmichael designed for Armstrong.

Bob Roll, *The Tour de France Companion: Victory Edition*. New York: Workman, 2004. A fully illustrated primer on the Tour de France, detailing its history, strategies, personalities, techniques, and much more.

John Wilcockson, *23 Days in July*. Cambridge, MA: Da Capo, 2004. An inside look at Lance Armstrong's record-breaking sixth consecutive Tour de France victory.

Les Woodland, *The Unknown Tour de France*. San Francisco: Cycle, 2000. A behind-the-scenes look at the Tour de France and how it has changed since 1903.

## Web Sites

**The Lance Armstrong Foundation** (www.laf.org). Official Web site of the organization that focuses on issues that people face in their battle with cancer.

**Le Tour de France** (www.letour.com). Official Web site of the legendary bike race.

**The Paceline** (www.thepaceline.com). Web site of the official fan club of Lance Armstrong and the United States Postal Service team.

**USA Cycling** (www.usacycling.org). Web site of USA Cycling, the official cycling organization recognized by the U.S. Olympic Committee.

**USPS Pro Cycling Team** (www.uspsprocycling.com). Official Web site of the United States Postal Service Pro Cycling Team.

# Works Consulted

## Books

Samuel Abt, *Lance Armstrong's Comeback from Cancer*. San Francisco: Van der Plas, 2000. A scrapbook of the Tour de France winner's dramatic career as one of history's best cyclists.

Lance Armstrong with Sally Jenkins, *Every Second Counts*. New York: Broadway, 2003. Armstrong's inspirational account of his victories in the Tour de France.

———, *It's Not About the Bike*. New York: G.P. Putnam's Sons, 2000. The best-selling autobiography of the cyclist, from birth through his first victory in the Tour de France.

## Periodicals

Samuel Abt, "The Big Show," *Bicycling Presents Lance Armstrong*.

"Armstrong Bid to Rewrite Tour History Overshadowed by Doping Claims," Agence France-Presse, July 2, 2004.

Todd Balf, "He's Back and He's Better," *Bicycling*, January/February 1998.

———, "Lance vs. Cancer," *Bicycling*, February 1997.

Chris Carmichael, "Armstrong Ready to Attack Mountains," Associated Press, July 11, 2003.

Nemil Dalal, "Cancer Panelists Inspire Packed Burnham Crowd," *Stanford Daily*, November 9, 2001.

Geoff Drake, "Lone Star," *Bicycling*, May 1993.

Rupert Guinness, "Armstrong Makes It Six; Boonen Wins On the Champs-Elysees," *VeloNews*, July 25, 2004.

Eric Hagerman, "Armstrong's Career Move," *Bicycling,* October 2003.

Sarah Kaufman, "Tour de Lance," *Washington Post,* July 26, 2004.

Ann Killion, "Historic Sixth: Armstrong Is Tour de France's Most-Celebrated Champion," *San Jose (CA) Mercury News,* July 26, 2004.

John Maher, "Proudly Following a Career from Afar," *Austin American-Statesman,* July 26, 1999.

Austin Murphy, "Tribute to a Champion," *Bicycling Presents Lance Armstrong,* Issue 43, pp. 12–16.

Peter Joffre Nye, "2nd Chance: The Cycle of Success," *Executive Update,* February 2002.

Shawn Pogatchnik, "Armstrong: An American in Paris Triumphs Again," *SouthCoast Today,* July 24, 2000.

Mark Riedy, "Sometimes It Is About the Bike," *Bicycling Presents Lance Armstrong,* Issue 43, pp. 97–107.

Linda Robertson, "With His Record Sixth Tour de France Title Secure, Lance Armstrong Enjoyed a Leisurely Ride Down the Champs-Elysees During the Event's Final Stage," *Miami Herald,* July 26, 2004.

Sal Ruibal, "Armstrong's Mother Always Part of His Team," *USA Today,* July 27, 2004.

———, "Armstrong Takes Victory Lap," *USA Today,* July 26, 2004.

Thomas Sancton, "From Despair to Glory," *Time,* July 19, 1999.

Michael Specter, "The Long Ride," *New Yorker,* July 15, 2002.

James Startt, "The Blue Train," *Bicycling,* October 2002.

———, "Lance's Tour," *Bicycling,* October 2001.

———, "The New Boss," *Bicycling,* October 2000.

Bill Strickland, "First Yellow," *Bicycling,* October 1999.

*Observer,* "Too Tough to Die," September 7, 2003.

Jeremy Whittle, "Armstrong Rides into History After Tour de Force," *The Times* (London), July 26, 2004.

## Internet Sources

Samuel Abt, "Cycling: Book Details Suspicions About Lance Armstrong and Drug Use," *International Herald Tribune,* June 14, 2004. www.iht.com/articles/524790.html.

"Armstrong Has the Hardest Choice After Easiest Tour," *Sports Illustrated,* July 26, 2004. www.si.com.

"Armstrong Rediscovers Joy of Cycling in Win," *Sports Illustrated,* July 25, 2004. www.si.com.

"Armstrong Second in Opening Event," ESPN, July 3, 2004. sports.espn.go.com.

"Armstrong Security Beefed Up After Threats," July 24, 2004, Agence France-Presse. www.keepmedia.com.

"Armstrong's New Trek Modeled on AMD 64-Bit Processors," *WTN News,* July 7, 2004, Wisconsin Technology Network. www.wistechnology.com

Alastair Campbell, "A Legend? I Would Rather Be Remembered as a Dad," *UK Times Online,* February 28, 2004. www.times online.co.uk.

Steve Donohue, "Riding Along with Lance," *Multichannel News,* June 21, 2004. htp://print.google.com/priint/doc?articleid=5fJS QtlcwA.

John Hoberman, "A Pharmacy on Wheels—the Tour de France Doping," MESO-Rx International. www.mesomorphosis.com/ articles/hoberman/tour.htm.

"Lance's Tour de Force," *Sports Illustrated,* July 25, 2004. www.si.com.

Ian Melvin, "The Armstrong Story—Part I," *Roadcycling,* July 1, 2003. www.roadcycling.com.

"My Way: Six and Counting for Armstrong," *Cycling News,* October 26, 2004. www.cyclingnews.com.

Dan Osipow, "Hold the Mayo . . . McEwen Takes the Lead," *Dan Osipow's Notebook,* July 6, 2004, United States Postal Service Pro Cycling Team. www.uspsprocycling.com.

———, "Pozzato Stays Strong in Final Sprint to Take Stage," Dan Osipow's Notebook, July 10, 2004, United States Postal Service Pro Cycling Team. www.uspsprocycling.com.

"Rivals Eagerly Await Post-Armstrong Era," *Sports Illustrated,* July 26, 2004. www.si.com.

"Testicular Cancer Treatments: Chemotherapy," Testicular Cancer Resource Center. tcrc.acor.org/chemo.html.

Jeremy Whittle, "Miracle Man." http://bicycle.szm.sk/lance.html.

# Index

# Picture Credits

Cover: Gero Breloer/DPA/Landov
AFP/Getty Images, 25
AP Wide World Photos, 10, 30, 36, 74
Bernd Thissen/DPA/Landov, 7
Cynthia Hunter/AFP/Getty Images, 22\
DPA/Landov, 88
Doug Pensinger/Getty Images, 60, 77
EPA/Landov, 57
Eric Gaillard/Reuters/Landov, 80
Frank Fife/AFP/Getty Images, 84
Gero Breloer/DPA/Landov, 58, 70, 78
Graham Chadwick/Getty Images, 55
Jason Reed/Reuters/Landov, 41
Jim Young/Reuters/Landov, 39
Joe Patronite/Getty Images, 19
Joe Raedle/Getty Images, 47
Joel Saget/Getty Images, 63
Michal Svacek/AFP/Getty Images, 87
Mike Powell/Allsports/Getty Images, 16
Mike Powell/Getty Images, 21, 29, 33, 44
Pablo Cocco/AFP/Getty Images, 48
Paul Buck/Getty Images, 64
PRNewsFoto/Bristol-Meyers Squibb Company, 83
PR NewsWire Discovery Channel, 91
Rellandini/Reuters/Landov, 69
Stephen Dunn/Getty Images, 13
Tom Able-Green/Getty Images, 51
Tony Barson/WireImage.com, 43

# About the Author

John F. Grabowski is a native of Brooklyn, New York. He holds a bachelor's degree in psychology from City College of New York and a master's degree in educational psychology from Teachers College, Columbia University. He has been a teacher for thirty-four years, as well as a freelance writer, specializing in the fields of sports, education, and comedy. His body of published work includes forty-eight books; a nationally syndicated sports column; consultation on several math textbooks; articles for newspapers, magazines, and the programs of professional sports teams; and comedy material sold to Jay Leno, Joan Rivers, Yakov Smirnoff, and numerous other comics. He and his wife, Patricia, live in Staten Island with their daughter, Elizabeth.